BOOK 2
ORGANISATIONAL PURPOSES AND OBJECTIVES

BOOK 3
ANALYSING EXTERNAL RELATIONSHIPS

BOOK 4
COMPETING WITH CAPABILITIES

MBA
Strategy

The Open University
BUSINESS SCHOOL

The Open University,
Walton Hall, Milton Keynes MK7 6AA

First published 2000. Reprinted 2001

Edited, designed and typeset by The Open University

Printed in the United Kingdom by Henry Ling Limited, The Dorset Press, Dorchester,
Dorset DT1 1HD

ISBN 0 7492 9835 9

Further information on Open University Business School courses may be obtained from
the Course Sales Development Centre, The Open University, PO Box 222, Milton Keynes
MK7 6YY (Telephone: 01908 653449).

1.3

19244B/b820b1-4i1.2

BOOK 1

INTRODUCTION

Author: Eric Cassells

CONTENTS

1 INTRODUCTION

1.1 THE COURSE

This is the first of eleven authored course books which form an important element of your learning on B820 *Strategy*. They complement other media such as the videos, audios, Set Book, Course Reader, face-to-face seminars, electronic conferencing, residential school, assignments, and case studies to form a whole. The books, along with the Set Book and Course Reader, provide much of the basic knowledge and understanding you need on the course. They do, however, go beyond this and ask you to apply that knowledge to real-life examples and case study situations, and to reflect on and challenge your understanding of strategy.

The course also goes beyond merely presenting frameworks for strategy analysis and planning. The techniques of strategy analysis have long been available on the open market. There is a constant testing of theories and models, developing new ideas, and discarding some that no longer seem so valuable. Mere knowledge of these models, techniques, frameworks and theories – however up-to-date and well-informed – cannot confer any advantage for you over any other manager who has chosen to be as well-informed. What is important is the way you use these techniques, the rigour and realism of your thinking when you use them, the innovation and insight you can bring to the process, and the quality of the arguments and conclusions you develop from the results of their use. The prime purpose of this course is, therefore, the improvement of the quality of your strategic thinking.

We discuss the key areas of strategy analysis and reflect upon many of the topics in strategy that we believe are most significant or are likely to become more important in coming years. We also seek to highlight apparent tensions or contradictions in the theories and models presented, so that you can understand their strengths and weaknesses, and so that you are aware that there are often many different explanations for observed phenomena in strategy. Finally, we highlight the essential ambiguity and uncertainty that is a precondition to making strategy. After all, strategy is about charting an unknown future.

1.1.1 The course content

The course begins with an introduction to strategy, and a discussion of what strategy is and why it is important. We take a first look at the different ways that strategy can be made, and what we mean by strategic thinking. This theme of strategic thinking recurs throughout the course as a way of coping imaginatively with complexity in managerial decision-making.

We next consider the role of collective purposes and objectives in driving strategy forward, and review the stakeholder approach to aligning interest groups with organisational objectives. The identification and management of stakeholder interests is another recurring theme in strategy.

To study this book you need:
  Course Reader

An extensive discussion follows of some of the most important thinking in competitive strategy. Reviewing the search for an effective match between an organisation and its environment, the discussion focuses particularly on the search for competitive advantage, and the uniqueness of an organisation's resources and capabilities as a key competitive weapon. The different ways in which organisations compete and the different bases for choosing strategy are described and analysed, first from an external perspective, and secondly from an internal organisational perspective.

This discussion of competitive strategies is extended into the areas of strategic innovation and strategic learning.

Strategy is also about how decisions are taken. A close look at the way that strategies form must therefore consider the importance of human cognition in decision-making, for example in the way in which problems are framed. The course gives attention to strategy as a process.

The discussion of process leads on to the theme of developing organisational capability for strategic effectiveness and advantage. It covers the four interrelated topic areas of organisational structure, systems, power and culture. Strategies are developed and implemented in organisational contexts which are not neutral. Changing the strategy usually implies change in structure, systems, power and culture. If you change the strategy without reviewing these other organisational variables, the strategy change has little chance of surviving.

Corporate strategy is the level of strategy which addresses the need for a corporation to develop capabilities in the selection of its portfolio of businesses and in continuing its disparate business units so as to add value. This theme is extended into a consideration of strategies used by corporations to pursue success across international borders. International strategy involves both additional complexity and opportunity. Multinational companies have to develop strategies for benefiting from the opportunities inherent in international operations, while at the same time coping with tremendous regulatory, financial, cultural and political pressures.

The course concludes by drawing together its main themes, and allowing you to reflect on what you have learned. Finally, it considers some of the challenges facing managers in finding effective strategies to deal with the future.

1.1.2 Aims and objectives of the course

B820 *Strategy* is designed to improve both your sensitivity to strategic issues and the quality of your strategic thinking. By the end of the course you should have a clearer perspective on your current or potential role in the strategy of your organisation, and of routes open to your organisation in pursuing superior performance. You are expected to:

- develop skills in the processes of thinking strategically – an awareness of what analysis, choice and implementation of strategy each require – through applied work on case material and investigations into your own organisation's strategic activities
- develop a high level of understanding of the concepts, theoretical ideas and empirical research findings which underpin the study and management practice of strategy

- challenge these concepts, theoretical ideas and empirical findings and develop your own views on the part which managers play in the making of strategy.

1.2 INTRODUCTION TO STRATEGY

This book introduces the course. In addition to setting the scene for your studies, it provides a brief introduction to a few important ideas in strategy.

First, in Section 2, we explain how an effective strategy can have a significant impact on an organisation's success through the creation of a dynamic match between the organisation and its environment, and how managers play a central role in making that happen. This is followed in Section 3 by a discussion of what strategy is. It identifies strategic issues to give you an idea of the topics that strategy deals with. This is further explored by a comparison of strategy with functional, technical or specialist management, which are more familiar levels for most managers. The book then considers in Section 4 the processes by which strategy is made or formed in organisations, drawing your attention to, for example, the differences between 'strategic planning' and 'strategy'. Finally, in Section 5 we start exploring the skills needed in strategic thinking, the capability which B820 takes as the prime focus for your development.

1.2.1 Learning objectives of this book

On completion of this book you should be able to:

- identify the features that set strategy apart from functional or specialist management
- identify the main features that characterise a strategic issue, and those issues that you believe to be strategic for your own organisation
- demonstrate the significance of an effective, dynamic, interactive and stretching fit between an organisation and its environment as a determinant of success, and appraise your own organisation against these criteria
- discuss the implications of defining strategy as either plans and intentions, or as a pattern of activities or actions
- examine critically the strategic recipes and approaches to strategic thinking employed in your organisation
- be aware of the need to develop a critical challenging approach to strategy reflecting the need for complexity and innovation in strategic thinking.

2 THE IMPORTANCE OF STRATEGY

This course is about those actions that determine whether an organisation survives, prospers, or dies. A consistent, coherent, effective and appropriate strategy is critical to the relative success of an organisation in its business over time, however we define 'success'. This applies to organisations in all sectors and industries, and regardless of the way strategy is made. Moreover, strategy is purposeful: managers at all levels have an important role in ensuring the survival and prosperity of the organisations for which they are responsible.

For managers, strategy involves a great many activities. Understanding those which make a difference to the success of an organisation is a key skill. Generally, managers should pursue strategy with consistency. They need to understand the challenge posed by their organisation's environment, and see how they can exploit the organisation's sources of advantage to best effect. In turn, this means that they should know the uniqueness and distinctiveness of their organisation, its resources and capabilities, the way it competes for scarce resources and custom for its services. Managers must be able to act on uncertain predictions of an unknown future, and seek out sources of innovation in the way their business operates and competes. Managers must also be able to implement effective change and to align collective objectives in their organisation to allow new capabilities and skills to be developed.

The importance of consistent, coherent, effective and appropriate strategy can be seen in the growth of pharmaceuticals giant Glaxo in its launch of the most successful drug in the world, Zantac.

MINI-CASE: BEATING TAGAMET – GLAXO'S STRATEGY FOR ZANTAC

By 1996, Glaxo had become the largest pharmaceutical company in the world, overtaking Merck through its acquisition of a major competitor, the Wellcome Foundation. In 1981, prior to the launch of its highly successful Zantac drug, Glaxo ranked twentieth by size in global pharmaceuticals. Glaxo's growth had been fuelled by the success of Zantac, the biggest selling drug in the industry, accounting for nearly 2 per cent of all drug sales worldwide, twice the amount of Merck's Renitec. Glaxo had already risen to become the second largest drug company on the organic growth of Zantac, and its rate of sales growth continued to outstrip competitors.

Yet the prospects for Zantac prior to launch were not outstanding. Zantac was a development of a group of anti-ulcerants called H-2 antagonists. Prior to 1976, the only treatment for stomach ulcers was the use of antacids for short-term pain relief, and of surgery for healing. In the early 1970s Smith Kline & French scientist Dr James Black discovered an H-2 antagonist which not only neutralised the effect of acid in the stomach (as antacids do), but also inhibited the production of more acid, and led (in most cases) to the healing of the ulcer without surgery. (Dr Black later received the 1988 Nobel prize for medicine for this breakthrough.) Smith Kline launched Tagamet in the UK in 1976. By 1982, the launch of Tagamet in Japan meant it was present in all major markets, and it had become the world's best selling ethical pharmaceutical product. At its competitive peak in 1981, Tagamet had 62 per cent of a worldwide market worth £600 million. It also had an excellent reputation amongst prescribing doctors as a safe, tried and trusted medicine.

On the discovery of Tagamet, Glaxo re-orientated its research efforts in anti-ulcerants to produce a similar compound with slight variations in chemical structure. To synthesise the drug after Tagamet's launch in 1976, Glaxo sped up their development process considerably. They significantly shortened the period required for clinical trials and gaining regulatory approval by adopting a parallel processing approach, with simultaneous clinical trials in 20 countries, and simultaneous presentation of their approval package in 26 countries in 1981. Glaxo then took the revolutionary step of sanctioning the building of the production plant prior to obtaining clinical approvals. The drug was launched simultaneously in all major markets in 1982, unlike the six years Smith Kline took to complete the global launch of Tagamet. This acceleration had two important effects. First, while Tagamet's market share may have seemed unassailable by 1982, a further three-year wait would only have enhanced Tagamet's market position. Secondly, by reducing the time from patent registration to the date when the drug could be sold for cash, Glaxo was effectively increasing the number of years in which the fixed-term patent could be exploited as a source of advantage in the market, thus increasing long-term cash inflows.

Analysts predicted little success for Zantac, however, with the most optimistic forecasts imagining maximum worldwide sales of £100 million per annum. Tagamet's market share, production economies of scale, and entrenched reputation with conservative prescribing doctors as a safe and effective drug were seen as insurmountable advantages. Zantac was widely seen as a 'me-too' product, insufficiently differentiated from Tagamet to overcome the latter's entrenched position. As a consequence, Glaxo's marketing department, armed with extensive market research, recommended a classic price-cutting follower strategy for Zantac. Zantac's launch price was to be 10 per cent less than that of Tagamet, whose high price was considered to be the maximum the market could bear. At this time, Glaxo was known for the quality of its research, but not for its commercial acumen, having previously failed to properly exploit exciting discoveries such as Ventolin. Glaxo's chairman, Sir Paul Girolami, disagreed with the marketing assessment. He believed it was essential that, if Zantac was to be perceived as a superior product, it had to be launched at a significant premium to Tagamet. Zantac was therefore launched at price premiums of 80 per cent (UK), 60 per cent (Germany), 50 per cent (France), and 20 per cent (the USA) over Tagamet, depending on the circumstances of each individual market.

What, however, was the basis of this perceived superiority? The apparent answer, according to the market research, was that Zantac had only marginally superior product features. Whereas US regulatory authorities had described Tagamet as a 'major therapeutic gain' over antacids and ulcer surgery, Zantac's approval came with a statement that it made 'little or no' additional contribution to existing therapies. Glaxo's marketing of Zantac made every use, however, of the minor differences that did exist between it and Tagamet – Zantac was marketed as an advance in anti-ulcer therapy. Launch promotion stressed the greater convenience for patients of a twice daily dosage (as compared with Tagamet's four times), and a four-week treatment cycle (six weeks for Tagamet). More important still were Glaxo's emphasis of its above-average reputation for research, and the potency and safety of Zantac. Prior to the launch of Zantac, Tagamet was seen as an extremely safe drug with a proven track record. Very few drug interactions had been noted, and side effects – which occurred in less than 1 per cent of cases – were not widely recognised by doctors. One of the proven occasional side effects, however, was gynaecomastia, a condition which gave rise to swollen and tender male breasts. In addition, there had been unproven speculative debate that Tagamet produced male impotence and reduced sperm count. Zantac's trials, however, had shown it to be 100 per cent free of side effects. Zantac's launch therefore stressed itself as a 'fast, *safe* and *specific*' advanced H-2 antagonist. This left it open for doctors to see Zantac as 'faster, safer and simpler' than Tagamet. All of this was aided by press cuttings that, for example, heralded Zantac as: 'a new anti-ulcer drug which does not affect people's sex lives' (*Oxford Mail*, 14 October).

Zantac's marketing led to a powerful, coherent position as the premium safe and effective anti-ulcer drug. This was reinforced post-launch when Glaxo sponsored conferences to promote research that showed Zantac had a 6 per cent higher healing rate in use, and a slightly lower one-year ulcer recurrence rate. These studies were further used to promote the idea of Zantac as an ongoing therapy to prevent recurrence with a reduced daily dosage. Glaxo virtually invented the post-healing market for anti-ulcer 'maintenance' treatment, changing the way doctors thought about ulcers from an acute, curable disease to a chronic, lifelong illness.

The third strand of Glaxo's successful marketing of Zantac concerned its early realisation that it would need alliances to ensure rapid promotion of Zantac globally. In particular, ethical drugs were heavily dependent on effective sales forces visiting prescribing doctors to promote usage. Glaxo had only partial worldwide coverage of major markets, and set up a variety of marketing alliances and licensing arrangements in countries such as Italy and France. The largest market in the world – the USA, with about 35 per cent of the anti-ulcer market – was targeted through a successful alliance with Hoffman La Roche, who already had an established sales force. This pragmatic approach to exploiting the limited life of a pharmaceutical patent enabled Glaxo to become a global pharmaceutical company very rapidly.

Smith Kline's defence of Tagamet proved ineffective ultimately, although it stressed the drug's safe history of usage. In particular, in the years following Zantac's launch, they reduced Tagamet's price and started to stress its price advantage, inadvertently reinforcing the perception of Zantac as a superior premium product. In 1986, Zantac overtook Tagamet sales worldwide, and became the first drug to sell more than $1 billion dollars annually. Other drugs were launched by competitors but, with the exception of Astra's Losec, rarely gained more than a few per cent of the market, being seen as 'me-too' products. By 1989, Zantac accounted for 42 per cent of the global anti-ulcerant market, twice that of Tagamet, with sales continuing to rise. Despite stronger competition, market share continued to rise to 44 per cent in 1992, with year-on-year sales growth still averaging 13 per cent (reflecting the ongoing growth of the total anti-ulcerant market from £600 million in 1981 to £5,114 million in 1992). By 1992, Zantac accounted for 44 per cent of Glaxo's group sales, and Glaxo had become the second largest pharmaceutical company in the world.

Sources: R. Angelmar and C. Pinson (1992 and 1993) 'Zantac (A)' *and* 'Zantac (B)', *INSEAD, Fontainebleau; J. Kay (1993)* Foundations of Corporate Success, *Oxford University Press, Oxford.*

Glaxo is one of the clearest cases of strategic success in the last twenty years. According to John Kay (1993), in his study of corporate success, it has added more value through its activities than any other company in Europe during that period.

Glaxo's success is probably mostly based on its ability to turn what were very minor product differences between Zantac and the entrenched competitor, Tagamet, into very large perceived differences in the minds of prescribing doctors. To some extent, it may be construed that Glaxo even created some of these perceived differences. Regardless of this, the company sent a very clear and consistent marketing message to doctors and rapidly built up a distinctive brand on the basis of its premium price and 'safe' image. This consistent message was carried by its advertising, pricing and packaging.

Another important aspect of Glaxo's successful strategy for Zantac was the company's innovative approach to product development and launch. This approach could be compared to the parallel engineering employed by Japanese car manufacturers. Glaxo's willingness to take some risks to circumvent a sequential development process saved them years of development time, which translated directly into additional patent earnings, as well as allowing an attack on Tagamet to be viable in the first place. In addition, Glaxo innovated to ensure the simultaneous launch of its product internationally. This showed an acute sense of the importance of competing in time in strategy, and the vision to break with traditional development and launch techniques.

This innovative streak did not, however, mean that Glaxo was unrealistic about the constraints that faced it. It understood fully the importance of sales forces as distribution channels, and knew it had weaknesses in this respect in many countries. Rather than embark, therefore, on a prolonged and costly effort to establish its own sales forces abroad, Glaxo utilised the skills and time advantage gained from a number of joint ventures. This appears to have been a successful decision given the advantage that Tagamet had from its entrenched position on the launch of Zantac.

The story of Glaxo and Zantac is therefore clearly one where a consistent, coherent, effective and appropriate strategy was central to their very great success in the period of the case. It is also a story of how managers can make a difference in strategy, with the notable story of how Sir Paul Girolami stood out against all accepted wisdom to position and price Zantac as a premium product – probably one of the most valuable decisions in business history. Remember, Zantac was not significantly superior pharmaceutically to Tagamet. The real difference was the way in which its strategy was developed and implemented.

Strategy and the purposeful strategic action of managers and entrepreneurs is also critical to the success of smaller businesses. Consider, for example, the case of Grapevine Records, a small London-based European record label.

Singer Emmylou Harris's career was boosted significantly when she signed with Grapevine Records, whose strategy was to carefully target the marketing, distribution and promotion of established artists neglected by the major record companies

MINI-CASE: A COWGIRL'S PRAYER – GRAPEVINE RECORDS

In early 1994, Emmylou Harris crowned a twenty year recording history with the US release of her most acclaimed album since her debut albums, 'Pieces of the Sky' and 'Elite Hotel'. The critical acclaim was matched by an upturn in Emmylou's commercial success in the US, as the album sold well beyond the confines of her loyal country and western following.

In Europe, however, the story was different. Emmylou's album, 'A Cowgirl's Prayer', languished unissued. Despite regular concerts in Europe, European sales had seen a gradual slide from her widespread popularity in the late 1970s to the point where a 1990 release sold just 7,000 copies. Her record label had gradually withdrawn promotional support, and eventually stopped distributing her new product there.

Emmylou signed her European distribution rights to the unknown Grapevine Records during the summer of 1994, and her new album was released six months after its US release. The album once more received critical acclaim, and sold 23,000 copies in its first year. By the end of 1995, Grapevine also released her Daniel Lanois produced follow up, 'Wrecking Ball', which went on to win record industry awards and bigger sales again.

Grapevine

Grapevine Records was founded in the UK in 1991 by Steve Fernie and Paddy Prendergast, when they started distributing Mary Black's albums. Both came from a music industry background: Steve working as a business manager with EMI Records and Paddy running a record manufacturing brokerage business.

Their decision to form Grapevine was based on their belief that there was a business opportunity in focusing on signing rock stars, famous in the 1960s and 1970s, but now largely written off by the major record companies. Record companies such as Warners and CBS concentrated on artists who could achieve high volume sales (threshold sales of 50,000 to 100,000 per annum). Grapevine's decision proved to be a success. By 1996, the company had built up a turnover of £3 million, signed up 14 acts (including Joan Baez, Janis Ian, Christy Moore and Graham Parker and the Rumour), had a catalogue of over 50 albums and a customer database numbering about 45,000.

Grapevine's initial strategy was to encourage yesterday's mega-stars to switch record labels. Under their existing contracts, many of the artists found themselves overlooked due to their low annual record sales volumes. Large company promotional budgets were spent on more fashionable acts. Grapevine offered the tangible benefits of increased sales and publicity, by carefully targeting the marketing, distribution and promotion of these artists. In addition to Emmylou Harris, another of their notable success stories were the Kinks. Under their previous record labels, album sales had been in the region of 5,000. On the Grapevine label, sales increased dramatically to 23,000.

As the company has developed, the key strands of their strategy have been to focus on:

- Signing up artists who still appear live and have a sizeable fan base.
- Actively building up and managing the database of fans for each artist. One method that has proved successful is putting fliers on seats at concerts.
- Gaining control of distribution. In 1993, Grapevine bought Rio Distribution from Polygram Records. The company was renamed Grapevine Distribution and, through control of its own sales force, it added a further valuable dimension to Grapevine.
- Developing a faithful following for artists' careers, as opposed to simply selling the latest record. Marketing and promotion efforts concentrate on establishing a long-term rapport with customers through targeted mailings, world-wide-web sites, competitions, discounts and concert promotions.

In 1995, Grapevine started to extend the scope of the business, venturing into complementary areas. In September 1995, the company launched a specialist reggae label, Vineyard. Following a similar pattern to the original Grapevine concept, the Vineyard label has already released six albums from artists such as Chaka Demus.

In another new development, Grapevine signed up five unsigned artists, including Sinéad Lohan from Ireland and Boston's Dar Williams. These artists were targeted because their music is likely to appeal to the existing

Grapevine customer database. Grapevine put together a 'sampler' record featuring several tracks from each of the new artists, to be promoted to 25,000 names specially selected from the customer database. This new development was potentially more lucrative for Grapevine, as they were able to negotiate much stronger contracts with these new artists. Traditionally the contracts negotiated with existing artists have been limited geographically and for short, fixed-term periods, whereas contracts with new artists are long-term and provide Grapevine with exclusive worldwide rights.

Conclusion

Grapevine is building a new business within a highly competitive and cut-throat industry. Grapevine has successfully identified and exploited a number of niches in the music industry, which do not seem to be considered viable for major record companies. Their success comes from targeted marketing and distribution, building up a catalogue of artists and a database of loyal career followers. The integration of marketing, distribution and promotion gives them an advantage over other small specialist independent record labels.

The main threat to Grapevine comes from natural fashion cycles within the music industry and from the artists themselves. To protect itself, Grapevine has concentrated on building up and sustaining the level of interest and the following of its artists amongst its customer database, making this proprietary asset valuable to its artists.

(Case prepared by Dorothy Cassells from interviews with Steve Fernie)

The story of Grapevine Records in the five years from its inception illustrates the success of a strategy based on exploiting distinct niches by focusing on targeted customers. The company has achieved much of its success by ensuring that its distribution channels work very effectively, and that there is a close relationship between the composition of their database of customers and the variety of products they offer. The company has shown an unusual awareness that it is the systematic refinement of this database that is probably the label's biggest single asset.

Grapevine's strategy also shows a keen awareness that its success is founded on the differences between it and the major record labels. This is not to say that a major record label could not have promoted Grapevine's artists as effectively, although, by 1996, the cost of building up such an effective customer database might make this prohibitive. The difference for Emmylou Harris and the other artists is that Grapevine were willing to give them attention and think innovatively about their futures. In being willing to invest in the rejuvenation of the careers of such 'mature' artists, Grapevine has also built a business for itself where others may have believed none existed.

The Grapevine story shows how coherent and innovative strategic thinking can be used to establish the businesses of entrepreneurs. Neither has this innovation stopped with their first business, but Grapevine have looked for opportunities to leverage their experience and customer database in search of new business opportunities.

Reflection

Consider the two mini-cases you have just read, Glaxo/Zantac and Grapevine Records. It should be clear to you that what was described was not functional or specialist management, but strategic management based on innovative strategic thinking. It would not have been possible in either example to achieve such a positive outcome without the senior managers in both companies deciding to exploit a unique opportunity. In many respects, both mini-cases illustrate strategies which went against the existing industry 'recipes' (see Section 5.2.1) and were, in part, counter-intuitive. Each also achieved their success within industries which are highly competitive. Consider too that although Glaxo was a large company, Grapevine was a tiny company set up from scratch by two entrepreneurs with an idea. In both big and small companies, the quality of the strategic thinking is more important than the size of resources. This should help you better understand the definitions of strategy discussed in the following section.

3 WHAT IS STRATEGY?

3.1   A DEFINITION OF STRATEGY

There are many definitions of strategy. You will find as many different definitions as there are textbooks. We could spend time reflecting on these, and debating the precise meaning of particular words and phrases. Much could be learned from such a study. We are, however, more concerned that you develop a meaningful understanding of what strategy is through your learning on the course. This includes your experience of using theories and concepts to understand cases and real-life situations, and of developing strategies.

This course takes a very broad perspective on the boundaries of strategy and therefore our definition is suitably broad:

> Strategy is the pattern of activities followed by an organisation in pursuit of its long-term purposes.

3.2   STRATEGIC ISSUES

A key skill for strategists to develop is the ability to recognise those issues facing an organisation that are strategic:

> Strategic issues can be characterised as developments inside or outside an organisation that are likely to have an important impact on its ability to meet or determine its purposes and objectives.

A helpful way of identifying strategic issues might be by reference to the military distinction between strategy and tactics:

- Military strategy is the holistic deployment of resources in a favourable position in a way that can influence the result of a war.
- Tactics are manoeuvres and actions utilised to win a battle.

For many managers, as for generals, the ease with which strategy and tactics can be distinguished on paper belies the difficulty of dealing with strategic issues and making decisions about strategy in practice:

> It may sound strange to say that more strength of will is required to make an important decision in strategy than in tactics. In the latter we are hurried on with the moment. A commander feels himself borne along in a strong current, against which he durst not contend without the most destructive consequences; he suppresses the rising fears and boldly ventures farther. In strategy ... there is more room allowed for our own apprehensions and those of others, for objections and remonstrances, consequently also for unreasonable regrets; and as we do not see things in strategy as we do at least half of them in tactics, but everything must be conjectured and assumed, the convictions produced are less powerful. The consequence is that most generals, when they should act, remain stuck fast in bewildering doubts.
>
> (Clausewitz, 1994, p. 21)

So the effective strategist is one who sees the significance of developments through the mist of current opinions and problems, is able to resist the temptation and diversion of the relative certainty of the tactical problem, and is able to act strategically in response to such key developments. This is precisely what Sir Paul Girolami did at Glaxo.

Activity 3.1

Create a list of those issues that you consider are the truly significant issues facing the organisation you work for at the present time, or one you know well. These will probably include developments arising both inside and outside your organisation. Are the issues truly strategic in that they have an 'important impact' on your organisation's 'ability to meet or determine its purposes'? Explain why the issues you identified meet these criteria for being strategic.

Experience is undoubtedly important in developing skills which will help you identify the strategic significance of an issue. In this course, we will ask you repeatedly to reflect on your own experience and history. We believe, however, that the skill of identifying key issues needs to be developed across a variety of contexts. Case studies and examples you encounter in the course, therefore, provide further practice in identifying strategic issues. It is important, also, that you follow the management and business press, to identify the strategic concerns of organisations today.

3.3 STRATEGIC CHOICES

The definitions of strategy and strategic issues above should help you to recognise when some of the choices you make as a manager are strategic. It is useful to identify the scope of the strategist's task:

> Strategy is concerned with the determination of the nature, domain and scope of an organisation's activities, and the evaluation of their success. The pattern of activities in strategy arises from the acquisition, allocation and commitment of a distinctive set of resources and capabilities by the organisation, in an effective match with the challenges of its environment, and from the management of the network of relationships with and between stakeholders.

Strategic choices are likely, therefore, to involve some or all of the following topics, and may be provoked by the types of questions suggested below.

Determining the nature, domain and scope of activities

What business is the organisation in, or in what sector is it active? What products or services does the organisation provide, and in what markets? How does the organisation provide its product or service? What are the skills, capabilities, and competences it utilises? Is it important that the organisation is different from its competitors? If a particular strategy is pursued, is it reversible?

Evaluating the success of activities

How does the organisation define success? Are measures of competitive advantage or superior profitability appropriate, or does the organisation pursue alternatives, such as efficiency and effectiveness? From what values and beliefs are its measures and definitions of success derived? What is the organisation's time horizon for achieving success? To what extent can the future be predicted when establishing targets for success? Can quantifiable measures of success be established? Will there be adequate and reliable information available to allow for the evaluation of success?

The acquisition, allocation and commitment of a distinctive set of resources and capabilities

How quickly must scarce resources and capabilities be replenished? If a new strategy is pursued, what new resources or capabilities will be required? Will these be acquired through purchase or internal development? How important are finance, skills, information, knowledge, or raw materials in the mix of resources required? Once committed, can resources or capabilities be recovered? What competing claims are there for resources? How should the organisation measure the effective use of these capabilities and resources?

Creating an effective match with the challenges of the environment

To what extent do the organisation's skills and resources match the needs of the environment? Can the organisation influence or change the environment? Which organisations does it compete with? Is the organisation like its competitors? To what extent does it rely on collaborators to provide skills, or elements of product offerings? How does it manage its boundaries?

Managing the network of relationships with and between its stakeholders

What objectives do the owners, financiers, employees, management, suppliers, customers and competitors have for the organisation? Are these in conflict? What is the balance of power amongst stakeholders? How significant are the resources each contributes? What is the influence of, for example, regulators, taxing authorities, planning bodies, politicians, voters, or the media?

Activity 3.2 _____

Consider an important strategic choice made by your organisation, at a level you are familiar with.

What were the underlying strategic issues or needs that the choice addressed. Which questions from the above section are helpful in defining the issue?

If you feel unable to identify an organisational strategic choice, you should consider a significant personal choice you have to make. These could include whether to accept a change of job or career, a decision to start a family, to move country or region, or how to start your own business.

Reflection _____

You should also reflect on the way the final choice was arrived at. Was it explicit and planned; an unrecorded decision made by an individual; a reaction to a single strategic issue; a decision made to meet operational or tactical needs, which nevertheless had strategic implications? Was there a clear objective when the decision was taken? Did the way that the decision was made affect the questions that were asked, the data collected, and, finally, the actual decision taken?

3.4   STRATEGY IS DISTINCTIVE

3.4.1   The shift from functional or specialist management

Strategy requires managers to adopt an organisation-wide perspective, together with a longer time horizon than normally applies in functional or specialist management. There are a number of ways in which strategy is distinctive when compared to the functional disciplines of finance, marketing, human resources, operations, information, etc., that you may have already studied. These are that:

- Strategy is *integrative and cross-functional.* You may be used to thinking of business problems as a functional or technical specialist. You may have been trained as an accountant, and be the financial controller of a medium-sized machine tools company. You may have classic brand management experience with a fast-moving consumer goods manufacturer, such as Nestlé or Procter and Gamble. You may be a scientist working in a government-funded nuclear physics research laboratory. You may be a doctor, holding a consultant position in a health service hospital. You may be a qualified information systems engineer working for a large bank. The perspective you have gained from such experience is immensely valuable, but it is not enough for the strategist. Strategy traverses traditional functional boundaries, and the management of relationships across the boundaries between organisational units is an important strategic task. Strategy requires an ability to retain a balanced vision of the role of all parts of the organisation in its overall business, while concentrating on those areas with strategic priority.

- Strategy concerns the *whole organisation interacting with its environment.* What happens in the environment affects the internal workings of the organisation, and vice versa. For example, if a competitor cuts prices across a range of products and the price cut was not matched, it would be likely that the organisation would need to make some volume cuts in production. Likewise, EU targets to cut back public borrowing as a percentage of gross domestic product might well lead to funding cutbacks in public-sector schools. Neither is an organisation passive. Therefore, a decision to expand into an overseas market may require a cross-functional approach to expansion inside the organisation: cultural acclimatisation and recruitment of staff; increased production; finance to fund the venture; information systems to provide management feedback and control; lawyers to deal with legal requirements; local tax experts; and a logistics system to ensure proper distribution. Finally, once these internal arrangements are made, it is unlikely that competitors in the overseas will simply sit back and let a competitor expand at will; they will fight back.

- Strategy has a *long time horizon* and is concerned with *projection and prediction of an uncertain future.* An organisation's past helps to determine the resources and capabilities available at any one time, but strategy's main interest is with predicting the future. Uncertainty comes from the unpredictability of the actions of other actors. These include governments who may alter regulatory regimes at short notice; customers whose needs may change, rendering products and services obsolete; existing competitors who may start to behave in unexpected ways; and unknown future competitors whose innovations could alter the nature of competition. The pace, variability, and dynamism of change does of course vary from sector to sector. For example, a monopoly supplier of regulated telecommunications services in a mature economy can probably predict revenues five years into the future with reasonable confidence. On the other hand, predictions of revenues from the supply of Internet navigation software or services must be open to considerable doubt.

Making strategy requires the assessment of information about the features of the organisation and its environment. This includes internal features such as operational, marketing and selling capabilities, and financial resources. External influences include the offensive or defensive stance of competitors, predictions for the growth of market sectors, the degree of concentration within an industry, and ideological influences on future government regulation. This process involves both identifying current trends and the more difficult task of spotting new trends, discontinuities and surprises.

3.4.2   The levels of strategy

Since making strategy demands cross-functional, integrative management of the whole organisation in its environment, some analysis of the levels at which strategy can exist within an organisation is required. Strategy is concerned with all levels, but it is helpful to create a classification that can help us focus our attention at any one time (see Figure 3.1):

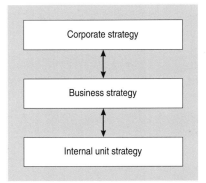

1   *Corporate strategy* – The management of the organisation's activities as a corporation, to gain maximum benefit from the combination of related or unrelated businesses.

2   *Business strategy* – Strategy in one business devoted to competing, for example, in an identifiable market-place, with a particular related product group, or using specific resources and capabilities.

3   *Internal unit strategy* – Within corporations and businesses, identifiable units are charged with technical, specialist, operational or functional tasks. These units need to have their own strategies for executing these functions or operations, and enlisting support from staff and other internal units.

Figure 3.1   The hierarchy of levels of strategy in an organisation

Strategy at any one level in the organisation is usually constrained by, and influences, strategies at other levels. For example, a production unit may be required to manufacture goods at 110 per cent of effective capacity to meet plans for selling in the market. As a result, the production unit will be unable to bid for any additional work which might be available, and the maintenance schedule for their machines may have to be accelerated to ensure smooth running.

3.5   STRATEGIC FIT

3.5.1   Strategic success and effective strategic fit

In the preceding sections, you may have noticed a recurring concern with the relationship between an organisation's environment and its internal resources and capabilities. This is a theme that underlies most thinking about strategy. A fundamental tenet of most thinking about strategy is that creating a 'match' or 'fit' between the organisation and its environment is essential to its relative success.

In Book 7 of the course, for example, you will encounter work by Mintzberg (1979), who identified five viable 'configurations' of organisational structure which arise to meet the needs of different environmental 'contingencies'. Mintzberg's study of organisations identified alternative types of strategic fit, without attempting to identify which of the alternatives might produce superior performance. Porter (1985) suggested that superior performance in business strategy, relative to other competitors in a market, comes from pursuing one of four distinct viable 'generic strategies', and excelling in it. These generic strategies will be described further in Book 5.

More recently, attention has focused on achieving competitive advantage and superior performance through the exploitation of opportunities in the environment using an organisation's unique set of resources and capabilities. This will be a significant theme of this course. For example, Kay (1993) asserts that:

> Corporate success is based on an effective match between the external relationships of a firm and its own distinctive capabilities.

Alternative perspectives on fit deny the significance of competitive advantage, however. 'Population ecology' (for example, Hannan and Freeman, 1988) emphasises fit as a long-term evolutionary process in highly competitive market-places. Darwinian selection means that inefficient organisations and managements fail when the environment changes. Equilibrium (or fit) between the *population* of organisations and their environments is maintained through the entry of new organisations and managers. In this view, fit may be maintained over the industry as a whole, but for the manager of an individual organisation there may be little that can be done: markets are not only harsh but difficult to anticipate, and attempts to adapt to new challenges may be fruitless. This may seem a pessimistic view of business as it emphasises the role of efficiency in determining those who are successful and survive, and suggests managers have little power to adapt their organisation to changes.

In the same way, neo-classical economics assumes competition is a process which acts to *homogenise* organisations and compete away advantages gained from differences in resources and capabilities. All organisations are driven to compete in the same manner (once again, on the basis of efficiency). Those organisations with significant efficiencies of scale tend to act as models for the consolidation of industries.

Strategy, however, projects a much more purposeful view of the role of management:

> ... the perspective is that of the management team assigned the responsibility of ensuring success, with success defined as either the entrepreneurial act of starting an organization, or those acts that condition survival.
>
> *(Rumelt et al., 1994, p. 39)*

The justification behind this purposeful strategic perspective lies in the simple observation that organisations are, in fact, *heterogeneous* within sectors and industries, competing in very many different ways. Managers *are* able to help determine the success of their organisations. This success is explained by the differences between the organisation and its competitors: differences in the unique set of resources and capabilities possessed, and differences in the way they compete within their environment.

3.5.2 Sustaining effective strategic fit

The goal of strategic fit between the organisation's distinctive resources and capabilities and its environment can seem seductively simple. Its simplistic application in strategy is, however, more likely to lead to long-term strategic failure than success. A sophisticated approach to strategic fit needs to account for the following factors:

- *The fit between the organisation and its environment is dynamic and interactive.* Whether an organisation can sustain the success that comes from its strategy will depend on how it develops its strategic resources and capabilities to meet the challenge of change. Pressures from the environment will vary from industry to industry and sector to sector, but observers discern some current common macro-environmental pressures (see Box 3.1). In addition, the competitive process means that competitors must be constantly outmanoeuvred: either a business makes its own advantage obsolete, or, eventually, a competitor will do it for them. Organisations should not, therefore, simply pursue 'fit' between the existing competitive environment and existing organisational capabilities. They should be anticipating environmental change, influencing the balance of forces in the environment, and developing their capabilities, resources and ambitions to underwrite new sources of advantage.

- Matching the organisation's resources and capabilities to the environment *does not imply an averaging process whereby all competitors,* using the same models and frameworks of strategic analysis, arrive at the same conclusions and *adopt the same strategies.* This is self-evident: customers do not have precisely the same needs or priorities, nor do they wish to pay the same price; and businesses have different capabilities and resources which enable them to interact with customer markets and segments in unique ways. So, an effective strategic fit will be one that utilises an organisation's distinctiveness in a unique interaction with a differentiated environment. This accords with advice of business consultants such as Bruce Henderson: 'Your most dangerous competitors are those that are most like you. The differences between you and your competitors are the basis of your advantage' (Henderson, 1989, pp. 139–143).

This second point highlights an important issue in your own study of strategy. The models, theories, concepts and frameworks you meet in studying this course cannot be a source of advantage in themselves if your competitors also have access to them. Models cannot substitute for the quality of strategic thinking. What is important is the way that you use the course frameworks as part of a critical and sophisticated approach to thinking about strategy.

BOX 3.1: CHANGE IN THE COMPETITIVE MILIEU

Some change occurs because of pressures from outside – from government, competitors, suppliers or customers. Other organisations change because owners, management or employees decide to change the nature of the business.

Many commentators have talked about the impact of change in organisations and the environment in recent years. For example, Prahalad and Hamel (1994) identify change in the 'competitive milieu' deriving from:

- *Deregulation and privatisation* – Profitability and patterns of competition in many industries have been altered dramatically by changes in government policy towards deregulation, e.g. airlines and telecommunications; and privatisation, e.g. the provision of public services through charitable bodies.

- *Structural changes to industries* – Previously concentrated industries, such as computing and information technology, have fragmented as technologies have changed.

- *Excess industry capacity* – A number of established industries such as consumer electronics and automobiles have been burdened by excess capacity at a time when developing countries have continued to add capacity.

- *Mergers and acquisitions* – These have been common in industries such as telecommunications and financial services as a means to access previously closed markets (such as public sector supply), to share the cost of research and development, or to rationalise capacity.

- *Environmental concerns* – Environmental safety and pollution liabilities affect most industries, and recycling and repackaging demands have altered the marketing of many products.

- *Less protectionism* – An ideological trend towards international free trade has been evident amongst many governments, and protected markets in telecommunications, power, agriculture, insurance, banking and retailing are being opened up to international competitors.

- *Changing customer expectations* – An increased concern for quality and demand for improved value has led to trends such as mass customisation, brand valuation, and the growth of direct selling.

- *Technological discontinuities* – New products can create new industries: cellular phones have expanded the telecommunications industry; biotechnology breakthroughs have changed the nature of some drug therapies; electronic conferencing and personal faxes allow telecommuting, and spawn products to support remote workers.

- *Global competition* – The old boundaries of domestic and international markets are laid open to question, as business ideas can increasingly be leveraged across international boundaries.

- *Emergence of trading blocs* – The breakdown of national economic boundaries has been accompanied by the grouping of countries into regional trading blocs such as the European Union (EU), North America Free Trade Agreement (NAFTA) and the Association of South East Asian Nations (ASEAN).

Reflection _____

Once again, we are asking you to consider the organisation you are most familiar with.

Has your organisation achieved a reasonable degree of fit with its environment? Do you consider that the way the organisation approaches the strategy of fit is inappropriate; is it too focused on internal or external issues; is the organisation too reactive, content to harvest its existing resources, capabilities and sources of advantage; is your organisation using strategy analysis in a way that leads to it adopting 'me-too' strategies that are too similar to its competitors? Alternatively, how does the organisation make use of its distinctive capabilities and resources in addressing the environment differently from its competitors?

Activity 3.3 _____

Now consider Box 3.1, and think of the pressures for change – both internal and external – which face your organisation. Prioritise these and other significant pressures which you feel are forcing strategic change on your organisation. What do you think are the implications of these pressures for your organisation's resources, capabilities and sources of advantage?

3.5.3   Strategic fit and strategic stretch

 Now read the article in the Course Reader by Gary Hamel and C.K. Prahalad entitled 'Strategy as stretch and leverage'.

This article challenges the simplistic application of the idea that success is related to effective strategic fit. Hamel and Prahalad review three elements: 'the concept of fit, or the relationship between the company and its competitive environment; the allocation of resources among competing investment opportunities; and a long-term perspective in which "patient money figures prominently."' They also make it clear that they agree with the importance of strategic fit as a determinant of success – ultimately. The central plank of their argument, however, is that 'fit' must be supplemented with the concept of 'stretch'.

A strategy of stretch applies where there is a significant gap between an organisation's resources and its ambitions and aspirations. In Hamel and Prahalad's opinion, it is this that has allowed apparently disadvantaged organisations such as Cable News Network and Komatsu to outmanoeuvre the entrenched advantages of sector giants such as CBS and Caterpillar. A strategy of stretch can be pursued in two steps:

1   Creating a 'chasm' between an organisation's resources and capabilities and its ambitions.

2   Bridging that chasm through the leverage of the limited resources and capabilities available.

This may sound trite, but Hamel and Prahalad's concern is with creating a sense of strategic leadership. It is also a difficult and risky strategy and two important qualifiers are highlighted:

1   The need to challenge the orthodoxy of accepted notions of ways to compete and operate.

2   The importance of managing this risk through acquiring detailed knowledge about competitors, customers, and capabilities in advance of the commitment of substantial resource allocations.

A great deal of Hamel and Prahalad's article is concerned with the leverage of resources and competences (or capabilities). This is particularly relevant both to your studies in Books 3, 4 and 5 where the focus is on managing external relationships and internal resources and capabilities at the level of business strategy, and in Book 9 when we will discuss corporate strategy.

The pursuit of a strategy of stretch is a challenging perspective, and a reminder that the relationship of fit between an organisation's capabilities and resources and its environment is a dynamic, interactive one.

4 HOW STRATEGY IS MADE

In some organisations, strategic decisions and choices are articulated through a strategic plan, with an action plan for implementing those decisions. Other organisations will have no strategic plan, but decisions will be taken and co-ordinated in the mind of one person – such as a small business owner. Alternatively, decisions may be taken in an unco-ordinated fashion, dealing with operational issues that also have strategic implications. Finally, it may often seem that organisations react to strategic situations and important issues without deciding anything beforehand. We explore many of these issues in depth in Book 6, but the following sub-sections suggest some variations in the ways that strategy is made.

4.1 STRATEGY BY PLANNING AND DESIGN

Many people associate strategy very closely with planning. Where strategic planning precedes strategic action, strategy could be characterised as:

> the adoption of a course of action planned through a linear process of analysis, formulation, and implementation.

The essentially linear, sequential nature of strategic planning is demonstrated by Figure 4.1, which maps out one approach to corporate strategy as recommended by Kenneth Andrews.

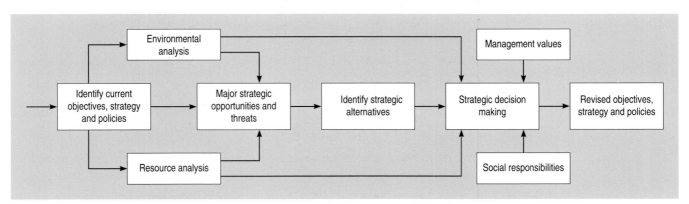

Figure 4.1   Andrews' recommendations for the corporate strategy process (Based on Andrews, 1971. Andrews never constructed an explicit flow diagram of his strategy formulation model. This diagram is based on the various ideas he presents in his text.)

Andrews' model, like most linear planning approaches, has the following key characteristics:

1   The recommended process directs you through a number of sequential, discrete activities.

2   The process begins with the identification (or clarification) of the organisation's current objectives.

3   Both the external environment and internal resources of the organisation are appraised.

4   Several alternative strategies are formulated.

5   At the selection stage, alternative strategies are evaluated against objectives, values and feasibility.

6   This strategic decision-making process results in the final selection of a strategy, which is followed by implementation.

Through this systematic, sequential approach, the strategy of the organisation is designed at one point in time, encouraging strategists to think holistically and develop an explicit sense of strategic direction.

Within this linear approach to strategy, a further distinction (Mintzberg, 1990) can be drawn as to whether the linear planning process is implicit or explicit:

- *Linear strategy by design* – This approach sees the making of strategy as the domain of top management, particularly of the chief executive or owner. This is a top-down, command-and-control approach where strategic decisions are made by top management, imposed on the organisation, and controlled through budgeting and reward systems. The image is of the strategist-general drawing on personal skill, craft, experience and intuition to analyse and formulate strategy.

- *Linear strategy by planning* – This approach encourages the making of strategy through a set of rational planning procedures. This is not necessarily a top-down process; a corporate plan can be the aggregation of separate business unit plans. Often, top-down and bottom-up processes intermingle. Nevertheless, the *process* is governed by best-practice and rational tools for analysis, formulation, and implementation. Such approaches are often evidenced by specialist planning units, or by explicit planning documents and policies.

Linear approaches to strategy and planning became popular in the 1960s and 1970s with the growth of large planning departments in companies such as General Electric and Exxon. Popularity has since waned (along with the size of planning departments). One criticism of planning approaches has been that, in practice, the process of analysis, formulation, and implementation rarely seems to take place in a linear, sequential fashion.

4.2   STRATEGY AS PATTERN

The sequential, linear approach often leads to a focus on explicit strategic intentions, clearly expressed prior to implementation. Strategy can, however, be made without explicit plans or without any clear prior intentions.

 Now read the article, 'Of strategies, deliberate and emergent', by Henry Mintzberg and Jim Waters, in the Course Reader.

This article highlights an important distinction between seeing *strategy as intentions or plans* and seeing *strategy as a pattern of actions*. For example, intentions in strategy may not be implemented in practice. Strategy can simply emerge as a clear, coherent pattern of actions with a consistent strategic purpose. Consider Figure 4.2, drawn from the Mintzberg and Waters article.

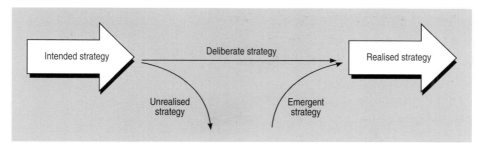

Figure 4.2   Making Strategy: deliberate and emergent strategy (Mintzberg and Waters, 1985)

We will consider strategic process in more detail in Book 6, but, for now, we can note the following about how strategy is made from Figure 4.2:

1   All strategy can be considered to be a pattern of actions.

2   Deliberate strategy is a pattern of actions where prior intentions or plans are realised (or implemented) successfully.

3   Emergent strategy is a pattern of actions where no prior strategic plan or intention exists. The actions emerge as a coherent pattern, however, and support consistent strategic purpose.

B820 is primarily concerned with strategy as it occurs, as a pattern of actions, whether it be deliberate or emergent. This does not mean we are unconcerned with the practice of strategic planning, merely that we do not restrict the scope of the course to planning.

5 STRATEGIC THINKING

5.1 STRATEGIC THINKING AND STRATEGIC DECISIONS

5.1.1 Strategic planning and strategic thinking

If you were taking a strategy course in the 1960s or 1970s, the chances are that the skills that we would be emphasising would be those of strategic planning. The early promise of strategic planning in the large corporate planning departments of General Electric, Shell and Du Pont has been replaced by more sober reflection on what skills are really needed to make strategy. Amongst all the possible skills, in B820 we choose to emphasise strategic thinking:

> There are no substitutes for strategic thinking. Improving quality is meaningless without knowing what kind of quality is relevant in competitive terms. Nurturing corporate culture is useless unless the culture is aligned with a company's approach to competing. Entrepreneurship unguided by a strategic perspective is much more likely to fail than succeed.
>
> ... Strategic thinking cannot occur only once a year, according to a rigid routine. It should inform a company's daily actions. Moreover, the information necessary for good strategic thinking is equally vital to running a business – designing marketing material, setting prices and delivery schedules, etc.
>
> ... There is a dangerous tendency today to practise single-issue management. The truth, of course, is that there is no easy answer. Quality, manufacturing, corporate culture, entrepreneurship, and strategic thinking are all important. Concern for one does not imply lack of concern for another. The most effective companies manage to integrate and make consistent all these aspects of management. ... One cannot ignore strategic thinking in favour of maintaining a supportive culture, just as one cannot ignore quality no matter how elegant is the strategic plan.
>
> *(Porter, 1987, pp. 24–25)*

This is not to say that strategic planning should be forgotten, merely that it is strategic thinking that matters. Planning can be an important process in encouraging and developing strategic thinking.

5.1.2 Information-processing, thinking and strategy

In considering the relevance of planning to the practice of strategic thinking, it is worth noting the impact of two different modes describing how managers mentally process information when making strategy (Walsh, 1995).

1   First, information can be processed in a *bottom-up* manner. This implies that strategic thinking will be driven by the process of gathering information. The strategist will examine all available information about a strategic problem or issue, review all possible

solutions, and make a decision after detailed consideration. This describes the idealised world of the strategic planner suggested in Figure 4.1, where information on current objectives, strategies and policies, the environment, and internal resources drives the identification of strategic alternatives and the choice of strategy.

2   *Top-down* information processing, on the other hand, is driven by the recall and application of theory and models to situations we encounter. In this case, theories about how the world works, or what kind of strategy will be successful, are built up by strategists from experience of the success of previous strategies. In practice, these theories are not elaborate; they are far more likely to be simple, abstract rules-of-thumb ('heuristics') or recipes for action.

In practice, the majority of strategic decisions are probably made using theories and models based on top-down information processing. This is because information can usually be processed more rapidly, and interpreting the current situation through models of past experience allows estimates to be made of the significance of missing information. The more routine and less novel a strategic decision, therefore, the more effective top-down approaches are likely to be.

Less routine and more novel strategic decisions may, however, render top-down processing based on models from past experience irrelevant or useless. Paradoxically, this does not necessarily mean that bottom-up information-processing will aid decision-making in more novel situations. The uncertainty and ambiguity which characterise less routine and more novel situations may simply make them more resistant to the analytical, information-gathering methods of bottom-up processing.

5.1.3   Uncertainty in making strategic decisions

Strategists are constantly faced with uncertainties in making strategic decisions. Often uncertainties simply reflect missing information. In other instances, uncertainty may result from the unknowable. Ambiguous information or contradictory outcomes from previous actions may also make the expected outcomes from a strategy uncertain.

Figure 5.1 considers the interaction of such uncertainties with the further uncertainties that may exist over the objectives of strategy in the first place (of which we will consider more in Book 2). The authors Earl and Hopwood (1980) use a matrix to categorise potential strategic decision-making strategies according to the types of uncertainty that exist over the objectives and/or the consequences of action.

| | Uncertainty over objectives for action | |
	Relative certainty	Relative uncertainty
Relative certainty	Computation	Bargaining
Relative uncertainty	Judgement	Inspiration

Figure 5.1   Uncertainty, objectives and action (Earl and Hopwood, 1980)

Figure 5.1 is a *contingency* model of decision-making which suggests appropriate strategies under different decision-making conditions. It takes the view that there is now one best way to make strategic decisions, but that decision-making should be tailored to the relative certainties management faces. This notion of contingency indecision-making should help you to make sense of the complex decision-making in which you participate, and to make more effective decisions as a result.

5.2 STRATEGIC RECIPES

According to J-C. Spender (1989), recipes of the kind involved in top-down information processing are guides to managerial action – frameworks made up of a number of heuristics and rules-of-thumb. When they are communicated between managers, they become the basis for shared organisational meanings, assumptions, and patterns of belief. Taken together, they then become a set of informal rules which explain expected outcomes of managerial action. For example, in order to maintain equilibrium with competitors in a market, a manager may follow these rules which together constitute a recipe:

- If a competitor does X, then we respond by doing A.
- If a competitor does Y, then we respond by doing B.
- If a competitor does Z, then we respond by doing A plus B.
- If we expect a competitor is thinking of doing X, then we prevent this by doing C.

Recipes are not closed statements which seek to provide general explanations, logically derived in the way that theories or models are. They are instead derived from managers' experience, observations and confirmations of expected action outcomes. Recipes are therefore open, providing principles to resolve problems and guide action, without being able to explain away or resolve all the uncertainties or ambiguities that surround such problems.

5.2.1 Strategic recipes and strategic change

Since recipes are derived from observing action outcomes, they are very context-specific. Different rules from the recipe are applied by managers as they encounter different situations: in a relatively mature market, price-cutting by a competitor will usually provoke aggressive counteraction to protect market share; in a fast-growing market for an evolving technologically advanced product, price-cutting may be interpreted as a sign of an inferior technology, and managers may ignore the competitor action as of no threat. Indeed, Anne Huff pointed out that many models and recipes actually derive in the first place from the *collective* experience of managers, rather than from individual experience. Such collective experience leads to the formulation of common recipes across particular contexts, such as an entire industry or sector (Huff, 1982; Spender, 1989).

There are significant implications derived from the observation that recipes are highly context-specific. The idea that they are derived from collective experience and observations, as shared meanings and assumptions, means that they are often seen as common-sense within that collective context. They are, therefore, taken for granted and rarely made explicit as part of a set of decision rules or protocols. Contexts – such as the bases of competition within an industry – change, however, and the effectiveness of recipes is undermined. The danger in recipes then becomes apparent. If they are taken-for-granted beliefs and assumptions which are implicit rather than explicit, they are rarely challenged. Outdated and ineffective recipes can outlive their relevance by many years. Consider, for example, the mini-case on F.W. Woolworth.

The strategies pursued by Woolworth's for over 40 years began to fail in the 1950s, but it was nearly 30 more years before drastic action was taken.

MINI-CASE – THE STRATEGIC SUCCESS AND DECLINE OF WOOLWORTH IN THE UK 1909–1982

Early growth and strategic success (1909–1950)

After initial success in the USA, F.W. Woolworth & Co. Ltd. ('Woolworth') entered the UK retailing market in 1909 with an innovative recipe for strategic success. Before their entry, UK shoppers were expected to select goods for purchase on the basis of window displays and prior knowledge of products. Once a customer entered a shop they were expected to make a purchase – to leave a shop without making a purchase was considered socially unacceptable.

Woolworth's revolutionary formula invited customers to enter the store and inspect the goods on offer, before having to decide to purchase anything. In addition, customers were offered a wide variety of goods at three fixed price points up to sixpence. The first Woolworth 'variety store' opened in Liverpool in 1909 and is said to have attracted 60,000 customers within two days.

There were four unusual operating principles that also contributed to Woolworth's phenomenal early success:

1 The company dealt directly with manufacturers, cutting out wholesalers' profits, and buying in bulk to achieve volume discounts.

2 All business was conducted in cash, to benefit from manufacturers' cash discount terms.

3 Store managers were given a high degree of autonomy to stock products they believed would sell in the local market.

4 Loyalty to Woolworth was all-important: all staff were promoted from within the company, learning the business in detail; long hours were the

norm; unionisation was not allowed; all managers were rewarded on results.

Woolworth's 'variety store' approach was a great success. The company grew dramatically and had 81 stores in the UK by 1918, opening a new store at the rate of one every eighteen days at one point. Furthermore, their growth was funded exclusively out of income from the UK operations, apart from the initial investment of £50,250 in 1909 – the only capital investment the US parent ever made in the UK. Woolworth understood its low-income customers thoroughly, and sales growth continued strongly throughout the three decades after its foundation. By 1939, 768 UK stores were owned, and two more operating principles were consolidated by this date:

5   All expansion was to be financed from profits, and no borrowing allowed.

6   All store properties were to be owned rather than leased or rented.

A period of stagnation in UK retailing followed during the Second World War and its immediate aftermath, as the UK government limited expansion and investment.

The strategic decline of Woolworth in the UK (1950– 1982)

After 1950, UK retailing changed dramatically as customers sought product quality and innovation after the austerity of the war, and as competitors introduced new retailing formats (notably self-service). The particular strategy that Woolworth brought to the UK in 1909, and which had fuelled its dramatic growth over 30 years, was no longer effective.

Woolworth continued to open stores (1,420 by 1961), but stuck to its existing 'variety store' competitive recipe. It developed a down-market image, and service continued to be based on sales assistants positioned behind fixed counters. While competitors limited the variety of the products they carried, Woolworth had difficulty controlling its duplicated product lines (up to 70,000 lines in the 1960s). Stock levels started to rise as the company concentrated on profit margin on sales, and ignored the turnover of stock. Woolworth's close relationship with suppliers camouflaged these problems of product line and stock control. The culture of internal promotion meant that managers often resisted new managerial and business ideas or innovations; senior posts were seen as rewards for long service. By 1968 the average Woolworth store made sales of £260,000, while Marks and Spencer – which overtook Woolworth as the largest UK retailer in that year – turned over an average of £1,300,000.

Realising that Woolworth's problems were deep-rooted, shareholders installed new top management in 1969, but progress till 1980 in rationalising product strategy and refurbishing store formats was painfully slow. Diversification was attempted by the management in 1980 with the acquisition of the B&Q home improvements chain.

In the same year, however, profits slumped badly to less than £1 million. By this stage the average sales from a Marks and Spencer store were eight times those of the average Woolworth site. The stock market valuation of the group was only £220 million while its property portfolio was valued at £500 million – the stock market believed Woolworth's competitive approach was actually destroying well over half the intrinsic value of its assets. Finally, institutional shareholders had become so disillusioned with Woolworth's management by 1982 that they established a consortium to acquire the company and install new management.

Conclusion

The 'variety store' strategy that brought so much success before 1950 became inappropriate and ineffective thereafter. A very successful strategic recipe which had originated in Woolworth in the early 1900s, based on the variety store concept and supplemented by the six major operating principles, became routinised and taken-for-granted as common sense in the company, but was overtaken by competitive events after 1950. The inappropriate recipe was so embedded in the company, however, that little challenge or fresh strategic thinking could take place for over thirty years. It was only when faced with failure that new management was introduced.

(Source: Gardner, 1995)

Activity 5.1 _____

Consider your own organisation.

1   To what extent can you identify a recipe that it follows in its operations or strategy? Are there particular ways of competing that are taken for granted as the basis of the organisation's success or survival – particular strategies that are accepted in a common-sense way by your colleagues as 'the way we compete' or simply 'the way we do things'?

2   Is there a recipe for competition that is common across the industry or sector? You may have worked for a competitor at some stage, other managers in your organisation may have worked elsewhere in the sector, or you may have come into contact with managers from competitors at trade seminars or conferences. To what extent do your competitors approach competition using the same recipes? Alternatively, are there differences in the way competitors approach markets which indicate that recipes are stronger at an organisational level?

3   If you work with colleagues who have a long history in the organisation, ask them what changes have occurred over the last 20 years in the way your organisation competes. Note, that if you are in the public or not-for-profit sectors, you should ask your colleagues about changes in the way your organisation competes for scarce resources such as funding or skilled labour. Do such changes indicate a change in the organisational, industry or sector recipe?

4   Finally, reflect on the degree of change in your industry or sector. To what extent do you think your organisation's ability to survive and prosper is compromised by a recipe that is no longer appropriate?

5.2.2   The need for fresh strategic thinking and innovation

Competing using organisational or industry recipes can provide effective responses to routine problems or existing modes of competition. To gain and sustain any long-term advantage over competitors, however, organisations may need to innovate. An important part of strategy revolves around the search for new ways to compete, or alter the basis of competition in an industry. In the same way, public-sector organisations may have to consider becoming involved in new activities to compete for resources such as funding, as the boundaries of public service provision change.

Existing industry or organisational recipes outline *existing* ways to compete. They may not provide any useful data where the environment changes significantly or suddenly. In addition, recipes tend to be based on the norm of past experiences; on encountering a similar (but different) strategic issue, the strategist may draw a reasonable (but inaccurate) inference from applying an old recipe. A company which has a very long record of successful innovation is Sony Corporation of Japan, which is discussed in the following mini-case.

MINI-CASE: SONY CORPORATION – INNOVATION AND STRATEGIC THINKING

Sony Corporation began in the years immediately after the Second World War. Its founder, Masaru Ibuka, described the challenge facing the diminutive Sony: 'We realised we could not compete against companies already in existence and against products in which they specialised. We started with the basic concept that we had to do something that no other company had done before.'

The Walkman and the Betamax video recorder were both products of Sony's strategy of innovation, but would Betamax have been more successful if a different, market-research led, strategy had been adopted?

The company's history thereafter is one of almost continuous product innovation – sometimes risking the entire company in order to promote a new product in which they believed. Many of these products were so innovative that they created new markets for customer needs which previously did not exist, such as the Sony Walkman which created the market for mobile personal musical entertainment.

By 1990, the company's name was believed to be the third most recognised brand in the world after Coca-Cola and Levi's. By 1994, the company recorded sales of £2.4 billion and had achieved a worldwide presence.

Over the 50 or so years since its incorporation, Sony's competitive innovations have revolved around competences in new technologies. One of the most significant of these was the 'Trinitron' colour television system – a system which competitors did not believe could work, let alone replace their 'shadow-mask' system, but which they have subsequently been trying to emulate since the late 1960s.

Product innovation has been matched by market innovations, the company repeatedly seeing possible new markets and unfilled, unrecognised customer needs. This ability converged most obviously with their innovations in product miniaturisation. Starting from an initial commitment to transistorisation and the development of pocket radios, through portable televisions, and Walkman tape and CD players, the corporation has shown an ability to lead the way in markets for mobile entertainment. While Sony undoubtedly needed research and development skills to develop these products, they also had the understanding and insight that there was an unfilled need for mobile entertainment – the ubiquitous sight of a jogger wired to earphones is a direct result of Sony's vision.

Sony's management was frequently criticised for taking irresponsible risks. Conventional management theory dictated that new products should be subject to extensive market research before they were introduced. Sony often failed to follow these conventions, pointing out that it is difficult to research a market for a radically new concept – how can people conceive of the new product in the first place?

Sony's main competitive failure in the introduction of new technologies involved the Betamax format of video tape recorder. This was an instance where the company's technological innovation was matched by an incomplete understanding of the competitive dynamics of the market they were creating. Although technically superior to Matsushita's alternative VHS format, Sony had not appreciated that successful introduction of the new product depended on the availability of Betamax format cassettes of adequate length for viewer playback. Regardless of technical superiority, customers bought more VHS recorders due to the widespread availability of two-hour VHS cassettes (twice the length of Betamax cassettes). In addition, Matsushita licensed manufacturers such as JVC and Phillips to make VHS recorders. This created a larger installed base of VHS recorders, which in turn made the format more attractive for pre-recorded tape manufacturers. By contrast, customers only had a limited choice of pre-recorded Betamax tapes, and eventually Sony was forced to withdraw their superior product.

(Source: this example is partly drawn from the case, 'Sony Corporation', by J.B. Quinn, in Mintzberg and Quinn, 1991, pp. 845–867, and from Quinn, 1992)

The mini-case noted how Sony's recipe for developing products did not include undertaking significant market research and as such was different from the *industry* recipe. This seems to have been a necessary precondition that allowed Sony's innovative capabilities to flower. Some of Sony's market innovations were indeed impossible to predict, and highlight the problems facing competitors in markets where sudden discontinuities occur; the continued dominance of the Sony Walkman/ Discman brands after 20 years in the personal mobile musical entertainment market is testament to this.

On the other hand, it is interesting to speculate whether a more complete understanding of the market-place could have led to the success of the Betamax video tape format. Would more extensive market research have anticipated customer needs more accurately than innovative insight? In this particular instance, the Sony recipe may have let it down.

Sony is a company built on competitive innovation. Its 50-year success story reflects a repeated ability to change the basis of competition through product and market innovation, thinking creatively about its strategy. The capabilities that Sony created over its history include the technological competences in developing innovative systems and in miniaturisation. Perhaps more important, however, was its capability for innovative strategic thinking, and anticipating and creating new product market-places.

5.3 INTEGRATION AND COMPLEXITY

5.3.1 The integrative challenge of strategic thinking

In Section 3, we noted that one of the factors that made strategy distinctive was its integrative nature. We shall now consider the complexity and scope of strategic integration:

> ... the management of strategic change involves consideration of not only the content of a chosen strategy, or even of the analytical process which reveals various content alternatives, but also the management of the process of change, and the contexts in which it occurs. Two aspects of context are considered: the inner and outer contexts of the firm. 'Inner context' refers to the structure, corporate culture and political context within the firm through which ideas for change have to proceed. Outer context refers to the economic, business, political and societal formations in which firms must operate. The process of change refers to the actions, reactions and interactions from the various interested parties as they seek to move the firm from its present to its future state.
>
> *(Pettigrew, 1988, p. 5)*

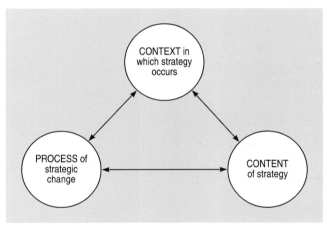

Figure 5.2   The scope of strategic thinking

The content, process and *context* of strategies help define the scope of strategic thinking. They are all closely connected and interrelated, and managers cannot consider one without understanding its interactions with the other two (see Figure 5.2).

In reviewing the scope of strategic thinking you should note that:

- There may be a temptation to emphasise action in the inner context, as this may seem more within the organisation's influence and control. Strategy does, indeed, involve actions to align information systems between functions such as marketing and finance, or to influence the norms or behaviours of individual employees. It also, however, involves actions to influence the outer context, alter the industry structure, lobby government to change regulations, influence society to make activities more acceptable, etc.

- Analysing the outer context involves the identification of the unique interaction of the organisation with its environment. Within this, it is useful to identify commonality between groups of organisations. For example, firms operating in the US market will face different environmental pressures from those in India; companies in service industries often require different technologies from product-based firms; and the political and institutional context of strategy in public-sector organisations is likely to vary from that in private firms.

- The impact of context must always be considered at all levels. For example, two firms may compete in the same heavily concentrated, cost-driven industry, and the outer industry context is therefore shared and similar. In thinking about inner context, however, those two firms may be structured internally around functional and divisional lines respectively, and may, therefore, use very different performance measures. The degree of similarity of context varies level by level.

While, for example, Shell and Exxon have traditionally competed within a very similar international outer context, internally Shell's structure has tended to favour the autonomy of national or regional management, while Exxon's structure has tended to emphasise functional or product lines of structure. These differences in inner context are likely to influence their strategies.

• There is a tension between developing your strategic skills in depth in a narrow context, and developing skills that enable you to bring strategic sensitivity to a range of contexts. Later in the course you will learn of the advantages and dangers that can simultaneously accrue to specialised context-specific assets and competences, and this will be an important consideration in your own career. For the purposes of this course, however, we expect you to develop sensitivity to a range of strategic contexts, via a variety of case studies and examples.

A simpler approach to understanding the complexity of strategic thinking is the proposition that strategy involves finding the answers to three questions:

1   Where are we now?

2   Where do we want to go?

3   How do we get there?

While these questions do not use the same terms that Pettigrew uses in the quotation above, they capture the same sense of the need to integrate thinking about strategy content, strategy processes over time, and the analysis of the inner and outer contexts of the organisation.

5.3.2   The complexity of strategic thinking

Strategic thinking is undoubtedly complex. It is highly integrative and involves a number of thinking skills. There are many dimensions that we could use to describe these skills. We have chosen to concentrate on just three of these in Figure 5.3.

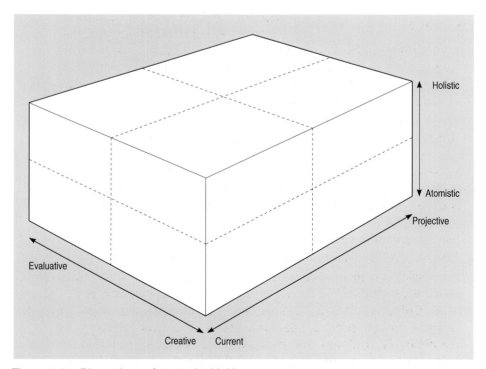

Figure 5.3   Dimensions of strategic thinking

Strategic thinking requires skills in many (and probably all) of the dimensions identified in Figure 5.3:

1 It should be holistic in its ability to integrate strategic concerns across the organisation. At the same time, it is important that the strategist simultaneously understands the strategic significance of issues at an atomistic (functional, technical, or unit) level.

2 Strategic thinking needs to identify the significance of current issues. It also needs to project strategy into the future, which is more problematical. Projection involves envisaging how a strategy will be implemented, predicting a whole range of possible actions and reactions from competitors and the macro-environment, and making calculations about uncertain cost–benefit outcomes of committing resources for future, long-term benefit.

3 Managers formulating strategy need to evaluate data and information, critically analysing issues and situations and predicting outcomes from existing knowledge and understanding. Equally, if a strategist hopes to accrue new competitive advantage, strategic thinking must be creative. Competitive innovation, as in the Glaxo, Grapevine or Sony mini-cases, means thinking of new, different ways to compete.

Examples of different modes of strategic thinking along these three dimensions are shown in Table 5.1.

Table 5.1 Examples across the range of strategic thinking			
Example	**Evaluative or Creative**	**Holistic or Atomistic**	**Current or Projective**
Interpreting departmental financial performance in the current period	evaluative	atomistic	current
Judging departmental financial resource requirements for a range of predictable outcomes	evaluative	atomistic	projective
Analysing integrated management information control systems in the current period	evaluative	holistic	current
Conducting a cross-functional resource requirement audit for a range of predictable outcomes	evaluative	holistic	projective
Reinterpreting current departmental cost allocations using a different accounting method (e.g. activity-based costing)	creative	atomistic	current
Designing an innovative accounting system that better measures future departmental performance (e.g. value accounting)	creative	atomistic	projective
Reinterpreting the current organisation as a network of distinctive competences and strategic relationships, rather than as a hierarchy of specialist functions	creative	holistic	current
Identifying innovative applications of existing competences that create new sources of competitive advantage	creative	holistic	projective

Activity 5.2 _____

Consider which different dimensions of strategic thinking you already use in your current employment. Using the three dimensions identified in Figure 5.3 and Table 5.1, list examples of strategic thinking modes you currently use. Try to identify examples from the eight different cells shown in Figure 5.3. It may be that it is relatively easy to identify situations where you have to be evaluative, atomistic and current in your thinking. On the other hand, it may well be that, at present, only more senior managers have the opportunity to be creative, holistic and projective in their thinking.

The importance of extending your strategic thinking skills should, however, be obvious. If superior performance within an industry or sector derives from a competitive advantage, the competitive process ensures that competitors are forever trying to erode your organisation's sources of advantage. Creating new sources of advantage drawing on your organisation's unique set of competences is a key skill for the strategist.

Think about any gaps in your experience of strategic thinking that this exercise highlights. During the period of this course, it would be helpful if you were to seek some experience of these different modes of strategic thinking. Alternatively, you may choose to talk to colleagues who have these experiences. What insights are they able to offer on the complexities that strategic thinking requires for their jobs?

_____

You will already have strengths in some or all of these dimensions of strategic thinking. We hope you will develop these further during the course and in your work. Some of the factors that will show the development of strong skills in strategic thinking are:

1   *The relevance and realism of your thinking* – For example, creativity is ultimately of little value if it has no real impact on strategy, or cannot be implemented or acted upon.

2   *The rigour of your thinking* – For example, a full understanding of all the opportunity costs and benefits of a strategic action.

3   *A varied approach to information processing* – You will use both bottom-up and top-down modes where appropriate, and will likely use both in combination.

4   *The use of theory to explain practice, and of practice to check the accuracy and relevance of theory* – You will use theory to add value to the analysis and description of a strategic issue, and will look at the available data from a strategic situation to challenge the usefulness of theory.

5   *A critical, challenging approach* – Theories, models and frameworks should not be taken for granted; judgement will be enhanced by knowing the strengths and weaknesses of these. You should consider the accuracy of information and data in an example or case.

Regardless of where your strengths currently lie, we believe you will develop your skills of strategic thinking through your studies on this course.

6 SUMMARY AND CONCLUSION

We have spent time in Book 1 explaining some of the conceptual ideas that help describe strategic thinking. Your real experience of this skill will come, however, in your practice of assessing case studies and applying ideas, theories and models from the course to your own experience of organisations and their strategy. The overriding impression of this theoretical material now, however, is probably one of complexity. Strategic thinking is not a straightforward skill acquired in one or two sessions. It develops over a lifetime of business and managerial experience.

Like strategic thinking, strategy is not easy. It is, however, at the very heart of organisational success. Strategy is a perspective on business that emphasises the differences between organisations. Organisations are not simply driven by the unrelenting forces of a perfect market towards the single solution of an unrelenting search for operational efficiency to secure survival. The survival of the fittest should not be construed as the survival of the most efficient. Efficiency is important, but strategy is about the fact that organisations are different. Organisations find a variety of ways to operate and compete for custom and scarce resources.

This variety provides an optimistic, if challenging, outlook for managers and business people. Strategy provides a perspective on business that emphasises strategic choice. In the differences between organisations lie the reasons why some are more successful than others. The set of distinctive resources and capabilities that a manager must manage and develop are the prime reason why any one organisation may achieve success or gain a source of advantage. Therefore, the strategic actions of managers are very important in the ongoing success of their organisations. Managers can make the difference between an organisation's death, survival, or prosperity.

Strategy is often talked about as the need to achieve a fit or match between an organisation and its environment. While 'fit' is, indeed, the prime way for an organisation to achieve success and survival, we recommend great care over the way that this term is employed. Fit will not guarantee success if it is static, or pictures the organisation as solely driven by reaction to the needs of the external environment. Neither will fit produce success if it is based on the same alignment of organisation and environment as the rest of the sector that your organisation operates in.

Strategic fit is a process. It is dynamic and constantly changing, recognising that strategy is about charting the course of an organisation in a shifting environment through time. Effective strategic fit must be interactive, where the organisation acts to influence and alter its environment. Effective strategic fit can only be a source of advantage if it is based on the unique relationship between an organisation's distinctive resources and capabilities and its environment. Finally, this dynamic fit should encourage the pursuit of new success and advantage: through the stretching and leverage of existing, and the development of new, resources and capabilities; and through innovation to find new ways to operate and compete.

REFERENCES

Andrews, K. (1971) *The Concept of Corporate Strategy*, Dow Jones-Irwin, Homewood, IL.

Clausewitz, K. von (1994) 'Art or science of strategy', in De Wit, B. and Meyer, R. *Strategy: process, content, context*, West Publishing, Minneapolis, MN.

Earl, M.J. and Hopwood, A.G. (1980), 'From management information to information management', in Lucas, H.C., Land, F.F., Lincoln, T.J. and Supper, K. (eds*) The Information Systems Environment*, North-Holland, Amsterdam.

Gardner, H. (1995) 'Rise, fall and regeneration', *Management Case Quarterly*, Vol. 1, No 1.

Grant, R.M. (1995) *Contemporary Strategy Analysis*, (2nd edn) Blackwell, Oxford (the Set Book).

Hannan, M.T. and Freeman, J. (1988) *Organizational Ecology*, Harvard University Press, Cambridge, MA.

Henderson, B.D. (1989) 'The origin of strategy', *Harvard Business Review*, November–December.

Huff, A.S. (1982) 'Industry influences on strategy reformulation', *Strategic Management Journal*, Vol. 3, pp. 119–131.

Kay, J. (1993) *Foundations of Corporate Success*, Oxford University Press, Oxford.

Mintzberg, H. (1979) *The Structuring of Organisations*, Prentice Hall, Hemel Hempstead.

Mintzberg, H. (1990) 'The design school: reconsidering the basic premises of strategic management', *IEEE Engineering Management Review*, Vol. 19, No. 3, pp. 85–102.

Mintzberg, H. and Quinn, J.B. (1991) *The Strategy Process*, Prentice Hall, Hemel Hempstead.

Mintzberg, H. and Waters, J.A. (1985) 'Of strategies, deliberate and emergent', *Strategic Management Journal*, Vol. 6, pp. 257–72.

Quinn, J.B. (1992) *Intelligent Enterprise*, The Free Press, New York.

Pettigrew, A.M. (1988) *The Management of Strategic Change*, Basil Blackwell, Oxford.

Porter, M.E. (1985) *Competitive Advantage: creating and sustaining superior performance*, The Free Press, New York.

Porter, M.E. (1987) 'The state of strategic thinking', *The Economist*, 23 May, pp. 21–28.

Prahalad, C.K. and Hamel, G. (1994) 'New strategy paradigms', *Strategic Management Journal*, Vol. 15, Special Issue.

Rumelt, R.P., Schendel, D.E. and Teece, D.J. (1994) *Fundamental Issues in Strategy*, Harvard Business School Press, Cambridge, MA.

Spender, J-C. (1989) *Industry Recipes: the nature and sources of management judgement*, Basil Blackwell, Oxford.

Walsh, J.P. (1995) 'Managerial and organizational cognition: notes from a trip down memory lane', *Organization Science*, Vol. 6, pp. 280–321.

ACKNOWLEDGEMENTS

Grateful acknowledgement is made to the following sources for permission to reproduce material in this book:

Text

Box 3.1: Prahalad, C. K. and Hamel, G. 1994, 'Strategy as a field of study: why search for a new paradigm', *Strategic Management Journal*, **15**, pp. 5–16, © 1994 by John Wiley & Sons, Ltd. Reprinted by permission of John Wiley & Sons Ltd.

Figures

Figure 4.2: Mintzberg, H. and Waters, J.A. 1985, 'Of strategies, deliberate and emergent', *Strategic Management Journal*, 6, pp. 257–272, Figure 1, © 1994 by John Wiley & Sons, Ltd. Reprinted by permission of John Wiley & Sons Ltd.

Figure 5.1: Arnold, J., Carsberg, B. and Scapens, R. 1980, *Topics in Management Accounting*, Figure 11.1, p.255, Philip Allan Publishers Ltd, by permission of Prentice Hall, UK.

Photographs

Page 12: Photo by Caroline Greyshock. Reproduced by permission of The Grapevine Label; *Page 31:* Reproduced by permission of Woolworths plc; *Page 34 (Walkman):* Reproduced by permission of Sony; *Page 34 (Betamax):* Mike Levers/Open University.

BOOK 2

ORGANISATIONAL PURPOSES AND OBJECTIVES

Author: Eric Cassells

MBA

Strategy

CONTENTS

1 INTRODUCTION

It is often remarked that successful strategy requires an organisation to find solutions to three questions: 'Where are we now?', 'Where do we want to go?', 'How do we get there?' A study of purposes and objectives in strategy might therefore concentrate solely on the answer to the question, 'Where do we want to go?' Such a book might discuss the setting of objectives to allow strategy to be implemented, and detail ways for performance targets to be established and measured. These activities are an important part of strategy, but in this book we discuss purposes and objectives in a broader strategic sense.

A consideration of purposes and objectives must also discuss the question, 'Where are we now?' This is important for at least two reasons. First, the current status of our organisation can tell us a lot about the activities that we like and dislike being involved in, the issues we consider important and worth pursuing, and the people we work with. Secondly, at any point in time, an organisation has built up a portfolio of skills, resources and capabilities. Where we want to go and what we want to do are critically dependent on what we have achieved to date, whether we can build on our skills or acquire new ones, and whether we are constrained by what we already do.

Taken at face value, the question, 'How do we get there?', implies a strong distinction between the ends that an organisation seeks and the means it follows to achieve those ends. For many people, however, what an organisation does is very important; the means can be the ends. In your own work, you may feel more willing to stay for long periods with an employer if you enjoy the work and develop your skills further as a result. On the other hand, it would be hard to imagine why a theatrical director would want to stay involved with a theatre if it decided to instead use its hall as a gambling casino. In the same way, entrepreneurs often enjoy the process of 'entrepreneuring' and the sense of achievement in establishing a new business idea. Once the business is established, however, they may have little further interest in it and move on to develop their next business venture.

In considering organisational purposes and objectives, we therefore have to acknowledge questions such as, 'Who are we?', 'Who do we want to be?', 'What do we hold to be important?', and 'What do we believe in?'. In this course we will not try to answer these questions for any specific organisation, but it is important for you as a manager to understand the answers for your own organisation. For your organisation, as for any other, understanding purposes and objectives depends on identifying collective and individual values and beliefs, cultural meanings and underlying assumptions (issues we look at in more depth in Book 8), and its sense of identity.

We must also resolve whether we believe an organisation exists as a separate entity, or whether it is merely an aggregation of individuals. This book assumes that organisations are collaborative devices with common collective purposes which are not necessarily identical to the purposes of individual members of the organisation. For individuals to remain members, however, there must be an acceptable alignment of individual

To study this book you need:
    Course Reader
    Set Book

and collective purposes and objectives, values and beliefs, and sense of identity. For example, the principle of 'cabinet government' often leads to individual government ministers defending policies they disagree with. Where ministers disagree with their government over issues they feel particularly strongly about, they will usually resign.

Stakeholder analysis will be a particular focus of this book. In establishing purposes and objectives, we recommend a pragmatic approach of determining the separate interests of stakeholders, recognising how these can be served, understanding the bases of their power, and identifying where confrontation and competition, or collaboration, are more appropriate relationship strategies. In addition, the book discusses the role of statements of purpose and objectives – such as missions and visions – in creating collective purpose, meaning and identity.

1.1   LEARNING OBJECTIVES OF THIS BOOK

After studying this book you should be able to:

- analyse statements of purpose and strategic rhetoric (such as mission statements), identifying the components of corporate purpose, objectives and strategy
- assess how influential your organisation's purposes and objectives are in shaping its strategy
- prepare stakeholder analyses which best describe the exchange and contractual nature of relationships between resource contributors and an organisation
- identify the power, interests and objectives of key stakeholder groups in an organisation
- review stakeholder relationships in your organisation to identify any mismatches between their contractual structure and the collaborative needs of the organisation (and its participants).

2 THE DEVELOPMENT OF AIRBUS INDUSTRIE

2.1 AIRBUS INDUSTRIE MINI-CASE

We start the discussion of purposes and objectives in strategy with a discussion of a mini-case drawn from the complex situation of Airbus Industrie, a commercial collaboration operating in a highly competitive market-place, but subject to significant government influence from four European countries.

MINI-CASE: AIRBUS INDUSTRIE

Why was Airbus established?

Airbus Industrie ('Airbus') was established under French law in 1970 as a Groupement d'Intérêt Économique (GIE – 'economic interest grouping'). It is effectively a joint venture between Aérospatiale of France (with a 37.9% interest), Deutsche Aerospace (37.9%), British Aerospace (20%), and CASA of Spain (4.2%). Since 1970 it has developed seven technically advanced airliner designs, serving 110 airlines worldwide. By the early 1990s it commanded a 30% share of the market in new airliners. In 1994, for the first time, it exceeded its main rival, Boeing of the USA, with nearly 40% of all new orders received.

The success of Airbus since 1970 masks the near total collapse of the European commercial aircraft industry prior to then. The aircraft industry is characterised by demands for large-scale commitments of resources, very large economies of scale, significant economies from experience and learning, and significant technological and learning synergies between the two main segments – military and commercial aircraft. Historically, the industry had been concentrated in Europe and the USA, with Europe often leading the way in technological innovation. The security concerns of the Second World War, the sustained period of Cold War confrontation between the Soviet Bloc and NATO, the US pursuit of the Cold War space race, and the heavy commitment of the USA to the Vietnam War, had, however, led the USA to place extremely large-scale orders for military aircraft with its home-based manufacturers.

The cross-synergies and scale and learning benefits achieved in the USA were substantial. The problem for European aircraft manufacturers is encapsulated by the levels of defence and space spending by the US government with US industry: over ten times that of the combined spending of the British and French governments. As a result, the average combined military and civil sales of the largest US aircraft firms (Boeing and McDonnell Douglas) were five times that of the largest European firms. The situation for European governments and manufacturers in 1970 was extreme: 'Faced with increasingly uneconomic national military markets and shrinking military exports, the major European industries either would have to increase their share of the civil transport market or would be reduced to a point at which competition with US firms would be out of the question' (Thornton, p. 29).

The interest of national governments in the civil aircraft industry is strategic for two reasons. First, air power has been the key military asset in modern warfare, and the synergies between military and commercial production are well-established. Secondly, the aircraft industry has encouraged the development of high value-added skills and technologies, employed large quantities of skilled labour, and there are many synergies with other high-technology industries; the failure of the industry would have knock-on effects on the economic power of the European nations.

The answer adopted by European governments and companies was to collaborate. Thus, Airbus was established to market and sell product lines of airliners, assembled from component sections supplied and manufactured by four constituent member companies. These partners were no longer capable of making complete civil airframes themselves. Much of the necessary development and launch funding came from the European governments involved, and it is unlikely Airbus would have existed without this aid. The aid was the subject of criticism and claims of unfair subsidy by Boeing and McDonnell Douglas, but Airbus retorted that this merely countered the implicit subsidy of the US government through its massive military spending.

To US competitors, Airbus's efforts in these early days were 'an anomaly', persisting 'in building, marketing and even designing new aircraft despite any apparent prospects of program profitability' (Thornton, p. 162). Indeed, from their entrenched position of scale and economic strength, Boeing and McDonnell Douglas paid little attention to the Airbus threat. It was only later that US companies realised that the Airbus strategy was essentially a 'mercantilist' one, where the interests of commerce followed those of national self-interest. Airbus was not governed by overriding objectives for maximising short- or long-term profitability, but for sustaining the survival of a European aerospace industry for national reasons.

The constraints on the management of Airbus

There were a number of important constraints on the strategic management of Airbus that arose from its purpose as a collaboration at a national strategic level to protect separate interests:

- The necessity of maintaining skills bases within each country, and the ongoing concern of the governments to continue with separate military aircraft capabilities, meant that production assembly lines were disaggregated. There was no single production line. Instead, fuselages, wings, and cockpits would be made in Germany, France, Britain and Spain, and flown in massive transport aircraft to Toulouse for final assembly. Boeing, on the other hand, built substantially all their airframes in Seattle.

- The objective of maintaining core national skills and employment bases meant that Airbus was required to source defined percentages of its main supplies from its owners, who were effectively guaranteed the roles of prime contractors in the design and manufacture of the airframes. Airbus was unable to utilise competitive markets for mainframe supplies.

- There was a conflict of interest between the partners' desire as owners of Airbus to see profits maximised and overall costs minimised, and their interest as suppliers in maximising their income from components supplied to Airbus. This conflict of interest made the task of creating an effective control system difficult.

- The GIE was responsible for the sales, marketing and after-sales support of the aircraft. Once more, the partners had a conflict of interest between their desire as owners that Airbus maximise sales, and their concern that Airbus might offer excessive price incentives to make such sales, thereby making their work as suppliers unprofitable.

- There was no transparency of accounting among the partners, and Airbus could not establish the true cost of its aircraft. Although there were efforts to introduce greater transparency of costs in the early 1990s, these foundered on the supplier/owners' desire to protect proprietary information about their cost structure.

- Airbus's legal structure as a GIE, the lack of sufficient partner incentive to restructure as a public limited company, and its dependence on the skills and technologies of its owners, meant that it was unable to raise commercial finance in its own right. Additionally, partner/owners were also often unable to agree on financing arrangements when their own finances were under pressure.

- The vast majority of employees working on Airbus aircraft remained contracted to the owners and partners, and considered themselves British Aerospace, Deutsche Aerospace, Aérospatiale, or CASA employees. Many felt accountable to their employers but not to Airbus.

At the core of the Airbus system to reconcile these conflicts and constraints was a set of contracting rules, which defined the precise portion of each aircraft built by each partner and the remuneration they received. The negotiation of these contracting rules took place before the building of each new product line, and reflected the partners' dual interests in maximising the reward they received for their own input, while reducing the overall cost of the aircraft to Airbus. Although true cost information was not available, Airbus made use of data on competitors' component prices and costs. This implicitly introduced a competitive effect to negotiation. At these negotiations Airbus acted as an important arbitrator of what the market could stand. The mechanism was reputedly self-regulating.

The challenge to the continuing success of Airbus

By the early 1990s, Airbus seemed to have established a successful collaborative approach, with an elaborate structure that recognised the realistic political and economic complexities that governed its existence. This structure recognised the national interests that created Airbus in the first place, and allowed the synergies and benefits of civil aircraft manufacture to benefit the individual national aircraft companies.

Airbus's commercial success in selling was built on a 20-year reputation for technologically innovative aircraft. In the early 1990s, however, Boeing had woken up to the challenge from Airbus. They started pursuing a relentless cost-reduction programme which re-engineered their manufacturing lines and drove down manufacturing costs by between 10 and 20 per cent. This cost advantage was translated into a very aggressive pricing policy. This stance, combined with a recession in the air travel market, led to increasing cost-consciousness on the part of airlines. As a result, Airbus's dominance of the market for new orders was short-lived: it plummeted from the near 40 per cent share in 1994 to only 19 per cent in 1995, behind both Boeing and McDonnell Douglas.

For ten years prior to this, British Aerospace had been arguing that Airbus should remake itself as an integrated commercial aircraft manufacturer in which the commercial air divisions of the owners were merged into one independent European entity. Airbus's success meant that it was now a bigger aircraft manufacturer than any of its owners, but national self-interest continued to make a true merger unlikely. The suggestion therefore foundered on the inability of governments and partners to agree such a major change. The substantial cost advantage that Boeing began to achieve by the mid-1990s meant, however, that Airbus had to consider moving towards single-site integrated manufacturing to continue to compete, as it was clear that its unusual structure drove up its cost base. In addition, it was proposed that Airbus must be free to source its components competitively on the open market, rather than being tied exclusively to owners as suppliers.

In addition to these commercial pressures, the geopolitical balance of power had altered dramatically with the collapse of the Soviet Bloc in Eastern Europe. The pressure on Airbus to change reflected the changed objectives of governments in the face of changed circumstances. In March 1996 the German government threatened to withhold any further subsidies for Airbus's key new project – the giant jumbo 'A3XX' – unless it was turned into a single integrated European company. According to Norbert Lammert, state secretary in the German Economics Ministry, 'co-operation among Europe's national aerospace companies was no longer sufficient to deal with US competition.' A report for the German government had criticised Airbus's 'loose structure', which 'tempted individual partner companies to put the strengthening of their own positions inside the consortium too much to the fore.'

(Sources: Thornton, 1995; Financial Times, *1993, 1994 and 20 March 1996;* International Business Week, *18 March 1996)*

Reflection

Consider the organisation you work for, or one that you are familiar with. To what extent do the purposes and objectives of multiple stakeholders place constraints on the strategies that the organisation can follow? Is there sufficient commonality between stakeholders' purposes and objectives to allow clear agreed organisational purposes to be established?

There are probably few organisations where managing purposes and objectives requires the management of the degree of complexity and constraint that Airbus faces. Does your organisation face such complexity in establishing and pursuing purposes and objectives? What difficulties do you and other managers experience in doing so?

2.2 AIRBUS AND THE COMPLEXITY OF MANAGING PURPOSES AND OBJECTIVES

The Airbus mini-case highlights many of the difficulties facing managers attempting to make sense of their organisation's objectives and purposes. Some of the difficulties that can be seen in the mini-case are:

* *Establishing and prioritising the organisation's purposes and objectives*
  In setting up Airbus, the owners and their respective governments had a variety of purposes in mind. A prime purpose was to save the European commercial aircraft industry from extinction. Underlying this, however, were a number of national 'strategic' rationales. Aircraft manufacture is an area of relatively sophisticated modern technology, with high value-added research and skills developed in the industry.

The economic activity, jobs, skills, and research and development capabilities associated with the industry were seen as important strategic assets by the governments involved. In addition, survival of the commercial aircraft industry was important to ensure the viability of an independent European military aircraft industry. In this sense, Airbus might even be thought of as an important part of national security policies, ensuring a credible European response to the military threat from the Soviet Bloc, and challenging the hegemony of US influence on the Western military alliance.

- *Understanding the relationships between, and the relative power of, stakeholders*

We have discussed the interests of governments in the Airbus collaboration, and there is little doubt that the Airbus venture would not exist without the launch and development aid offered by the German, French, UK and Spanish governments. What, however, of the interests of the owner companies? Deutsche Aerospace, Aérospatiale, British Aerospace and CASA have interests in Airbus making money as a venture in its own right. In addition, the long-term survival of their own independent businesses probably also depends on the skills and synergies gained in participating in the Airbus venture. Finally, the companies also act as suppliers and, as such, have an interest in achieving the best price for the supply of their own components to Airbus. The owners, therefore, have a number of conflicts of interest between their roles as owners and suppliers. Reconciling these interests is never going to be easy.

In addition to these conflicts, we can speculate about the interests of airline customers. It is likely that, for example, Lufthansa, KLM, American Airlines, Alitalia, and Iberia all benefit from the technological innovations Airbus has offered over its history. For instance, Airbus's 'fly-by-wire' technology allowed considerable automation of the flying operation in the cockpit. Equally, Boeing has begun to establish a position of low-cost based price dominance, which is also highly relevant to airline buying decisions. There are also considerable operational and maintenance savings from standardising the types of aircraft used by an airline. In addition to these purchasing and operational considerations, however, airlines have a strategic reason to ensure the survival of Airbus: should Boeing emerge as the sole supplier to the commercial airline industry, it is likely to exercise monopoly powers. How much, therefore, are the airlines prepared to pay to ensure the survival of other manufacturers, and to encourage competition based on both price and technological innovation?

In addition to the purposes and objectives of governments, owners, suppliers, and customers, a full consideration of stakeholder power would have to review the position of employees and managers in both Airbus and its owner-suppliers.

- *Setting up negotiation and conflict resolution mechanisms to reconcile stakeholder differences*

In order for Airbus to function as a commercial entity it has needed to develop elaborate negotiation procedures to reconcile the competing claims of its owner-suppliers. Complex agreements are reached prior to the development of new aircraft to allow projects to proceed on agreed bases. These negotiations are hampered in Airbus by the complete lack of information about an aircraft's cost structures, buried as this knowledge is in the records of its owner-suppliers. Here, however, Airbus has developed the technique of benchmarking the price of supplies against the open market. In recent years, too, governments have used the threat of the withdrawal of launch aid as a negotiating weapon to pressurise the owners into restructuring Airbus's activities. All of this, however, indicates that managers working in Airbus must be prepared to accept the highly political nature of their jobs.

● *Purposes and objectives which constrain organisational structures and control*

Airbus's purpose as a collaboration of separate manufacturers – all of whom wish to maintain their independence and skill base – means that it has been unable to pursue the kind of manufacturing economies which its competitors gain from integrated production lines. With wings being built in the UK and shipped to Toulouse for assembly, it seems inevitable that Airbus's cost base will leave it at a competitive disadvantage. Indeed, these cost pressures are such that Airbus, its owners, and governments are being forced to reconsider its very purposes – only political action will allow Airbus's purposes to be explicitly altered, so that structural change can take place. In addition, the lack of costing information available to Airbus for control is itself a result of Airbus's objective of maintaining independent aircraft manufacturers in each country involved.

2.3 SUMMARY

The above are just a selection of the complexities faced by Airbus in managing organisational purposes and objectives. All organisations are faced, likewise, with the need to reconcile purposes and objectives with activities through the strategies they adopt. Managers in public-sector organisations will, for example, recognise the difficulties of managing complex and conflicting stakeholder objectives. Managers in publicly quoted companies may need to meet targets of returns on shareholder capital, and may find that structuring diverse activities as distinct 'strategic business units' facilitates this. All of us, therefore, need to analyse and understand the impact of purposes and objectives on the strategies our organisations follow.

The Airbus case also highlights how important it is to understand the true purposes of an organisation and its competitors. According to Thornton (1995), Boeing and McDonnell Douglas assumed that Airbus was governed by the same objectives of making a commercial profit on each product line introduced. Understanding the significance of experience and scale economies, the US companies did not, therefore, regard Airbus as a serious threat for nearly twenty years. This delay allowed Airbus to establish a significant position in the aircraft industry. Airbus's persistence would, however, have been better anticipated had the US companies understood the venture's purpose as an important part of European national strategic and military policy.

3 STRATEGY, PURPOSES AND OBJECTIVES

3.1 'PURPOSES' AND 'OBJECTIVES' IN THE ORGANISATION

Before going further in our discussion of purposes and objectives, it will be useful to define some terms. You have already discovered in Book 1 that the way the word 'strategy' is used can vary significantly. Discussion of organisational purposes and objectives is also fraught with problems of terminology. In this area, you will often come across words such as 'vision', 'values', 'mission', 'objectives', 'aims', 'goals', often with conflicting meanings conveyed by the same word.

Activity 3.1 _____

Consider the use of words in an organisation with which you are familiar. List the words that you hear used to describe organisational purposes and objectives. If you can recognise an order of importance or priority in the terms, place them in that rank order. Wherever possible place an agreed organisational definition of what the word means alongside. If this is not possible, place a definition that captures your understanding of its meaning alongside. Looking over this list, can you see an obvious pattern or order? Alternatively, do members of your organisation use the terms in an almost random way?

Discussion _____

From our experience, there are two extremes of usage and definition. In the first, terms will be used without any agreed definition and reflect a variety of personal experience. In the second, there are likely to be agreed organisational definitions for the terms used. There is also likely to be an accepted hierarchical order depending on how general objectives are, how measurable or quantifiable they are, and the time horizon for their achievement. For example, a firm may have a published 'mission statement' ('to be the number one supplier of personal computer network maintenance services to medium-sized enterprises'), from which broad 'goals' are set ('to be the number one supplier in three important markets within three years'), and narrower 'objectives' cascade down ('to be the number two supplier in the USA and Australia within two years and number one in Europe within one year'). While this cascading order of terms may be dubbed 'mission, goals and objectives' in one firm, it is as likely to be termed 'vision, objectives and goals' in another.

3.2 THE MEANING OF 'PURPOSES' AND 'OBJECTIVES'

For this course, we use the following broad meanings when talking about organisational purposes and objectives:

- *Purposes* – Purposes reflect the values and beliefs of the main stakeholders, recognise the organisational culture and reflect the politics of stakeholder relationships. Purpose statements may take the form of a unifying vision, mission, or values summary, and ideally should capture the *raison d'être* and sense of identity of the organisation. They are likely to be general and long-term in nature. Such statements are less likely to provide quantifiable measures of success or failure.

- *Objectives* – Objectives are more specific than purposes. They express particular expectations of stakeholder groups, or specify particular milestones of achievement to be aimed at. Objectives are more likely to be quantifiable. Success or failure can therefore be more easily measured against statements of objectives. Statements of objectives are likely to be explicit in formal strategic planning processes.

3.2.1   The role of 'policy'

It is also useful to consider the role of policy in strategy. We defined strategy in Book 1 as a pattern of activities and, in our discussion of the role of intentions in strategy, we drew a distinction between *deliberate* and *emergent* patterns of strategy.

- *Policies* – Derive from an intention that a particular pattern of strategy will be implemented over time in pursuit of agreed organisational purposes and objectives. Policies can therefore lay out a programme for activities over a period of time. They can also provide decision rules to allow a consistent or measured response to any recurring contingency that is encountered. Policies therefore eliminate the need for recurring decisions, provide a systematic way of delegating responsibility to a lower managerial level, and encourage consistency in strategy. The relationship between these concepts is shown in Figure 3.1.

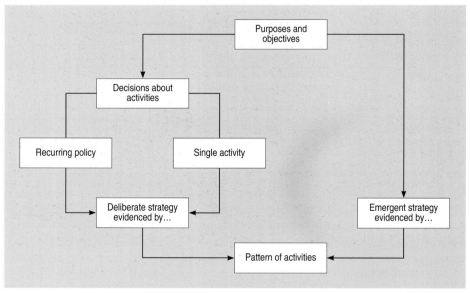

Figure 3.1 Organisational purposes, objectives, policies and activities

Example: NASA and the moon

The USA was surprised on 12th April 1961 by the ability of the Soviet Union to launch a human into orbit around the earth. The 'space race' was a symbol of the technological, political, and economic Cold War struggle between the two countries and the USA was clearly falling behind.

Yuri Gagarin's first manned space flight galvanised US political will into a clear visionary *purpose* for its NASA space exploration agency: that of landing a man on the moon before the Soviet Union. This purpose was translated into a measurable *objective* by US President Kennedy on 25 May 1961, with his pledge that the USA would land a man on the moon before the end of the decade (1970). Although NASA consumed an unusually large portion of US gross domestic product during the 1960s, it still had to make decisions about scarce resources (money and skills), as the task set by Kennedy was substantial. The US pursuit of the objective of landing a man on the moon was so overriding that *policy* decisions were taken to do little about another major aspect of space exploration – the building of orbiting space stations. US space launches, thereafter, were driven by the needs of the moon landing objective, and the Apollo lunar programme consumed most of NASA's resources until Neil Armstrong walked on the moon. The USA clearly beat the Soviet Union to the moon, but the consequences of their clear purpose, objective, and policy choices were as much evident in their success in 1969, as in the launch of the first orbiting manned space station by the Soviet Union in the early 1970s.

Russia's Mir space station photographed from the space shuttle Discovery during their rendezvous in January 1994. Although the USA beat the Soviet Union in the 'space race' of the 1960s, the Soviets had a successful strategy to build a manned space station.

3.3 PURPOSE AS PUBLIC STATEMENT

Understanding an organisation's purposes and objectives is an important first step in understanding its behaviour, including its competitive behaviour. Managers should therefore study what is written about their organisation's or a competitor's *raison d'être*, to identify as much as possible about its values, beliefs, meanings and assumptions, and sense of identity.

The most accessible form of statement of organisational purpose can be found in the published reports and accounts of large businesses. Often called 'missions', 'vision', 'guiding principles', or 'corporate profile', some examples of these follow in Table 3.1. These statements may be written to communicate the values, beliefs, and the strategic direction of the organisation and its people. They often also define objectives and broad action plans for strategy.

Table 3.1   Extracts from public mission and purpose statements

Save the Children Fund (written communication to the author)	Save the Children works to achieve lasting benefits for children within the communities in which they live by influencing policy and practice based on its experience and study in different parts of the world. In all of its work Save the Children endeavours to make a reality of children's rights.
Nokia (1993 Report)	Nokia has always achieved its greatest success by applying new technology with spirit and boldness.[...] recognising our shared values of *customer satisfaction, respect for the individual, achievement* and *continuous learning.*
British Steel (1994 Report)	British Steel intends to remain one of the world's leading steel companies, providing its customers with quality products and a level of service to meet their requirements whilst maintaining its internationally competitive cost base. In this way British Steel will endeavour to provide proper returns to its shareholders and to fulfil the aspirations of its employees and the communities in which it operates.
L.L. Bean (magazine advertisement, quoted in Grant, 1991, p. 24)	The Golden Rule of L.L. Bean: Sell good merchandise at a reasonable profit, treat your customers like human beings, and they'll always come back for more.
Glaxo (1994 Report)	Glaxo is an integrated research-based group of companies whose corporate purpose is to create, discover, develop, manufacture and market throughout the world safe, effective medicines of the highest quality which will bring benefits to patients through improved longevity and quality of life, and to society in general through economic value.
Fujitsu (1994 Report)	Our world is undergoing profound change as we race toward the 21st century. The technologies that support us are also advancing dramatically. Networking, open systems, rightsizing, and multimedia are the key words and technologies that symbolise today's world of computers and communications. They are the key words of the advanced information society, a society made possible by dreams and exciting technology. Fujitsu makes tomorrow's dreams come true today; with total computer and telecommunications systems based on leading-edge electronic devices. Fujitsu remains committed to capturing the future by offering optimal systems and high-quality services that will propel customers into the next century.

Médecins sans Frontières (charter, telephone interview)	Médecins sans Frontières offers assistance to populations in distress, to victims of natural or man-made disasters, and to victims of armed conflict, without discrimination and irrespective of race, religion, creed or political affiliation. Médecins sans Frontières observes strict neutrality and impartiality in the name of universal medical ethics and the right to humanitarian assistance and demands full and unhindered freedom in the exercise of its functions.
	Médecins sans Frontières volunteers undertake to respect their professional code of ethics and to maintain complete independence from all political, economic and religious power. As volunteers, members are aware of the risks and dangers of the missions they undertake and have no right to compensation for themselves or their beneficiaries other than that which Médecins sans Frontières is able to afford them.
Wal-Mart (1994 Report)	For more than three decades, Wal-Mart has delivered to customers quality merchandise at a low price. Always. At the same time, the Company has responded to the highly competitive, rapidly changing retail business. The Company embraces change and adapts whenever and wherever necessary. At Wal-Mart 'always' and 'change' – at first glance dissimilar concepts – form a dynamic partnership.

3.4 THE COMPONENTS OF PURPOSE STATEMENTS

Pearce (1982) analysed the content of missions, and identified the following components:

- Product or service, market, and production and delivery technology.
- Company goals: survival through sustained growth and profitability.
- Company philosophy, or statement of basic beliefs, values, aspirations and priorities.
- Company self-concept, or understanding of its place in its environment and its position relative to competitors.
- Present and future public image of company.
- Attitude to insider and outsider 'claimants', interest groups, or stakeholders.

Not all the components were found in all company missions analysed.

Activity 3.2 _____

Which of these components can you identify in the eight examples in Table 3.1? As an example, consider the statement (charter) of Médecins sans Frontières. This gives a clear indication of the product or service it is supplying, and the scope of the beneficiary (claimant) groups it is targeting. There is much about its philosophy and values of impartial assistance, and there is a particular concern that its public image as a neutral, apolitical organisation is explicitly recognised. This concern is presumably directed at ensuring that government stakeholders or other authorities do not impede the delivery of aid, and that funding can be gained from a variety of sources. The charter also deals specifically with establishing an understanding of risk with its volunteers.

You should be able to identify all six of Pearce's components at least once in Table 3.1, but some, such as stakeholders, products and technologies, recur. If your own organisation has a mission or purposes statement, repeat the exercise. If your own organisation does not have such a statement, you should instead develop a mission for it, drawing on and prioritising Pearce's components.

3.5 PURPOSE AND SOCIAL RESPONSIBILITY

Statements of purpose usually take account of the objectives of stakeholders or claimants. They often include a recognition of what Pearce called 'outsider' claimants, including society at large and governments in particular. In most cases, organisations want to demonstrate their good citizenship by showing socially responsible attitudes. The sixth largest retail bank in Britain, the Co-operative Bank, has even used its ethical stance for marketing – 'what makes us different is that we will not use your money to invest in corrupt and oppressive regimes.'

Published purpose statements have tended to focus on a number of high-profile social concerns such as environmental pollution, equal opportunity personnel policies, restricting investment in foreign regimes considered socially unacceptable (such as South Africa during the period of apartheid), funding educational initiatives, and the ethics of business in less developed economies. A particular concern in recent years has been the establishment of ethical principles for conducting business – although these initiatives often fall foul of the cultural complexity of ethical and moral schemes in the many different nations in which an organisation has to operate. Such issues will be discussed further in Book 8.

Of course, for many organisations operating in government or the public sectors, or in charities, there is an expectation that purpose and objectives will be closely connected to themes of social or national responsibility. Their ability to acquire resources may be very closely connected to meeting the social, national or charitable purposes they were set up for. Thus, for example, the published priorities for the UK's Department of Health (which is responsible, among other things, for the National Health Service) are:

- to protect, promote and improve the health of the nation
- to secure high quality health care through the National Health Service
- to enable the United Kingdom to play an effective part in the work of the European Community and other international health issues.
  (Department of Health, 1993 Report)

It would be too easy to dismiss social purposes as the domain of public-sector and charitable bodies alone: these complex concerns impinge on all organisations. The degree to which social themes figure in the purpose statements of an organisation will depend on:

1 the extent to which social issues matter to particular groups of stakeholders; and

2   the relative power of those stakeholder groups, and the importance of the resources they contribute.

A particularly strong example of social responsibility playing a prominent part in the identity and purposes of a commercial organisation, is that of the Body Shop chain of bodycare retail outlets. You will hear more about this company in the audio tape accompanying Book 8.

Example: regulation, social responsibility and banks

Almost all nations have regulated banking sectors. Banks have little choice but to recognise the social responsibilities imposed on them, whether or not this is reflected in official purpose statements. Regulation is usually enforced through licensing, detailed regulation and compliance procedures, and active regulatory and investigative bodies. Regulation is imposed by governments and recognises the centrality of the banking system in most economies. A prime purpose of regulation is to protect individual depositors from loss. Arguably more important, however, is the responsibility to maintain stability in a system which will allow a bank to lend up to twenty times the value of its underpinning financial capital.

A major goal of legislation is to fight crime by preventing the organised 'laundering' of criminal funds through the banking system, such as occurred in the failed Bank of Credit and Commerce International's US branch. Regulation, however, creates commercial opportunities, and some countries have sought to attract financial service suppliers through banking secrecy laws. An international bank, therefore, has to recognise that certain branches have to reflect the overriding legal requirement to protect the identity of depositors (as in Switzerland), while other branches must be seen to collaborate with authorities more concerned with establishing the legality of sources of funds (such as in the USA).

Reflection

Consider a private-sector company you are familiar with. To what extent does this organisation have purposes or objectives that involve social concerns and responsibilities? Are these stated explicitly?

In your opinion is the organisation serious about the pursuit of these objectives? How do these social purposes compare with the actual behaviour of employees? Consider how they interact with other purposes and objectives – are these social concerns central to the purposes of the company, or are they more in the nature of constraints on securing additional profits? What evidence exists about the real motives of the company in stating such social objectives?

3.6   CREATING A SENSE OF PURPOSE

'I would agree that unless our mission statement is backed up by specific objectives and strategies, the words become meaningless, but I also believe that our objectives and strategies are far more likely to be acted upon when there exists a prior statement of belief from which specific plans and action flow.'

(H.B. Atwater, Jr, CEO of General Mills, quoted in David, 1989)

Formal purpose statements may, unfortunately, fail to say much of substance about an organisation's values, beliefs, or strategic direction.

The need for each organisation to find its own sense of purpose, and the danger of unthinking adherence to 'best practice' in writing a mission, is captured by Eberhard von Kuenheim, Chairman of BMW:

> Last year marked a turning point. We had to bid farewell to almost a decade of steady growth in the German automobile industry. At the same time, we had to stop talking in generalizations and, thus, in over-simplifications, of our sector of industry [...] it became clear that this particular industry was at last developing in different directions. Today, we find successful and less successful manufacturers and suppliers in every country, in every region.
>
> The quest for panaceas, which in any case was doomed to failure, has ended. Strategies that proved successful in one country, or for one company, cannot be imposed upon another. Individual companies still have to analyse carefully these strategies for themselves. They must then decide whether such strategies can help them achieve their goals. Unquestioning adoption can be dangerous.
>
> In this situation, each company must define, and then hold to, its own way. [...]
>
> A common interest throughout the Company, in the thoughts and deeds of all its employees, has become more important than ever. We should not expect outside help. There are no examples to follow. A vain search for precedents would divert us from our chosen path.
>
> *(BMW, 1992 Report)*

What we are calling 'a sense of purpose' has been discussed by Andrew Campbell and Sally Yeung in their work on 'creating a sense of mission'. They propose a model of congruence between organisational strategy, purpose, values and behaviour standards to support a strong mission.

 You should now read their article in the Course Reader.

Campbell and Yeung say that a strong, clear mission can be a significant advantage for organisations and firms in pursuing success. Further, a strong, clear mission will only arise when there is a match between the 'emotional, moral and ethical rationale' represented by the organisation's purpose and values, and its 'commercial rationale' pursued through its strategy and behaviour standards.

Reflection

Considering the experience of your own organisation or others you are familiar with, do you recognise evidence to support Campbell and Yeung's case? Has your organisation achieved a reasonable degree of congruence between its strategy, purpose, values and behaviour standards?

Perhaps more controversially, the authors also suggest that success is best served when a 'sense of mission' is created through congruence between an employee's personal values and the organisation's values, and suggest that recruitment and personnel policies should recognise this. You may disagree with this approach on ethical grounds, but you might consider whether you believe it would be practicable in the organisation you are considering.

3.7 ORGANISATIONAL PURPOSES AND THE LANGUAGE OF STRATEGY

In this section we have discussed the problem of how language is used to define an organisation's purposes and objectives. In particular, we noted that many organisations will use different words to stand for purposes and objectives, and suggested that it was important that you established the meaning of the words your organisation uses. Further, we noted the advice of the chief executives of General Mills and BMW that the words found in a purpose or mission statement must have meaning for each individual organisation.

Eccles and Nohria (1992) applied ideas from language studies to strategy and management. While it is not solely about purpose and objective statements, many of their examples are drawn from missions and visions.

They suggest that an organisation's language (or 'rhetoric') has a direct impact on both its strategic actions and its collective sense of identity and meaning. They suggest that effective strategic rhetoric – including purpose and mission statements – provides meaning for an organisation's past and a sense of purpose as to its future. Effective rhetoric is an important strategic tool for building consensus to pursue collective strategic action. The results of action in turn impact on an organisation's sense of identity and its future strategic rhetoric. This argument presents strategy as an iterative, evolutionary process where effective rhetoric creates 'robust' strategic action, which in turn helps an organisation's sense of identity (and meaning) and probably alters its rhetoric. They offer this model not as a prescription for the way that rhetoric should be used, but rather as a description of the way that rhetoric actually influences strategy. They hope it will help managers to understand the relationship between the rhetoric of, for example, purpose statements and strategies.

In particular, the article quoted looks at the case of General Electric (the American multinational company) and note how the very language of the tools used by strategists – in this case, the language of portfolio planning – can be used by managers to create a sense of meaning around very diverse activities. This is a problem faced by many highly diversified conglomerate organisations. The success of simplifying rhetoric in creating meaning for its activities was, in turn, used by Jack Welch at General Electric to allow outsiders and managers to understand the direction in which the organisation was moving. The rhetoric and sense of meaning facilitated the creation of an agenda for collective action in what had become a rambling, incoherent structure.

In the case of Biogen, the authors look at the way strategic rhetoric both influenced the strategic routes taken by the organisation as it developed, and the way that the rhetoric was itself changed as the strategy evolved. Biogen was initially established under Wally Gilbert to 'pursue a broad range of commercial applications of *biotechnology*.' It became necessary, however, to establish a more focused identity as a *bio-pharmaceutical* company when the company's broad strategy threatened its very survival in 1985. With this change, both the chief executive and the strategic rhetoric changed, as did the strategic actions to develop a major 'blockbuster' AIDS treatment based on bio-engineering. Finally, the inability to capitalise on CD4 and the almost coincidental development of the synthetically produced anti-blood clotting drug Hirulog, led to another unexpected change of strategy. This time, Biogen's identity was redefined using the rhetoric of a 'global *research-based pharmaceutical* company'.

Throughout the Biogen story, the authors suggest that the choice of rhetoric and strategic action was 'path-dependent', that is it was conditioned by the decisions and actions the company took earlier in its history. Thus, the ability to transform Biogen into a synthetic pharmaceutical company could only have occurred because of the earlier decision to allow scientists 20 per cent unallocated time to pursue their own interests regardless of how they fitted with the company's stated identity. This particular strategy derived from Biogen's earliest identity as a collection of individuals pursuing their own interests in the broad field of biotechnology, and recognised the importance of the human skills and knowledge brought to its research activities. This strategy also implicitly recognised the need to establish a collective sense of organisational identity which was attractive to, and aligned with, the identities of its key research staff.

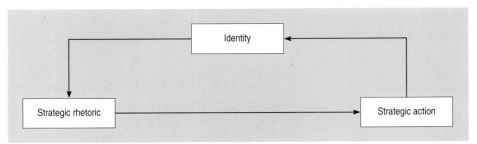

Figure 3.2   An action perspective in strategy and identity (based on Eccles and Nohria, 1992)

The authors bring their model together in a process diagram (see Figure 3.2) which suggests how collective and individual organisational purpose ('identity'), the language of purpose ('strategic rhetoric') and the strategies pursued ('strategic action') interact with each other over time in an evolutionary process, such as occurred at Biogen. Finally, they suggest that managers need to be aware of the rhetorical nature of vision, mission and purpose statements, in a sceptical way. This means being aware that the language of purpose can be used to support one particular view of strategy over another. In addition, it means being aware that this language can also provide the necessary sense of consensual purpose to support collective action in the first place.

4 MANAGING THE PURPOSES AND OBJECTIVES OF STAKEHOLDERS

In Section 3 we noted that Pearce (1982) identified the attitude to 'insider' and 'outsider' claimants as typical components of an organisation's mission. These claimants include executive officers, the board of directors, shareholders, employees, customers, suppliers, governments, unions, competitors, local committees, and the general public. In addition, the research of Andrew Campbell and Sally Yeung identified three types of organisations, where the interests of shareholders, stakeholders, or 'a higher ideal' were given prominence.

This section of the book will consider the purposes and objectives of stakeholders, including shareholders. We consider that it is impossible to determine the purposes and objectives of the organisation without first considering the collective positions of its interest groups.

4.1 IDENTIFYING STAKEHOLDERS

4.1.1 The nature of the stakeholder relationship

An organisation is a system for adding value through the acquisition, allocation and commitment of resources, drawing on a network of contributing participants. Stakeholders bring different resources to the organisation and an organisation's ability to prosper and survive depends on its ability to continue attracting those stakeholder resources, by adding value to them.

Stakeholders contribute resources in the full expectation of claiming some reward from the organisation's value-adding activities. Indeed, stakeholder analyses might be termed 'contributor and claimant' analyses. Stakeholder relationships are characterised by interdependence and exchange, a process of flux and mutual adjustment.

The possible reasons for participating in an organisation's activities have been categorised by Etzioni (1971):

1   Coercion, where participants are forced into contributing resource to the organisation (for example, a prison labour gang or conscripted military unit).

2   Mutually beneficial exchange, where participants receive a tangible, material benefit in return for resources (for example, a worker supplying labour in exchange for a salary or wage).

3   Identification with the organisation's values, norms, or beliefs (for example, a religious community or campaigning pressure group).

We most often think of organisational relationships as concerning the exchange of material benefits in an economic market-place. There is no reason, however, why organisational relationships cannot be founded on other exchanges. In coercive relationships, resource is contributed in exchange for the withholding of force or punishment. For example, as taxpayers we are all coerced through the threat of legal sanction into contributing financial resources to our public-sector service organisations. In markets where competitors collaborate to maintain price levels, they are often avoiding costly price wars for market share. Equally, it can be argued that lower wage levels in the charitable sector are a result of workers foregoing material reward for satisfaction or fulfilment of personal beliefs or values through charitable work.

4.1.2 The stakeholder framework

One of the most common tools for reviewing organisational relationships is the stakeholder framework. This maps out the relationships between stakeholders or participants in the organisation. Consider Figure 4.1.

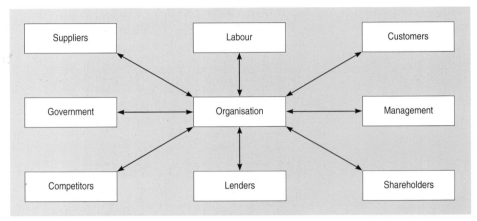

Figure 4.1 Simplified stakeholder diagram

The strategic concern for organisations is not merely with drawing a stakeholder diagram. It is with managing relationships, ensuring resources are obtained by the organisation, and that stakeholder claims are met. These relationships, resources and claims can be external or internal to the organisation. Indeed, the task of managing the boundary of the organisation is part of managing these relationships, and the precise location of the boundary is unlikely to be the same in each organisation.

4.2 MANAGING STAKEHOLDER OBJECTIVES – SHAREHOLDERS AND OWNERS

One way of simplifying the complexity of purpose statements accounting for stakeholder interests is to concentrate on the economic goals of shareholders or other equity participants in ownership. This approach is justified on the grounds that shares normally confer ownership rights. In the same way as you may see no reason why squatters, burglars or estate agents should benefit from the risks of ownership you accept when you buy a home and equip it with possessions, so an organisation may argue that owners should be the sole beneficiaries of its economic returns. Even where account is taken of other stakeholders, there is usually acceptance that residual benefits and profits should flow to the legal owners. Examples of published statements where companies identify strongly with the needs of their owners are shown in Table 4.1.

Table 4.1   Economic welfare of owners

Foster's (1994 Report)	Foster's Brewing Group has a number of aims and business objectives under the overall banner of enhancing shareholder value, including: • Ongoing cost reductions and productivity improvements. • Product innovation linked to consumer preference. • Product quality and technical pre-eminence. • Marketing excellence. • The ongoing orderly divestment of non-core assets. • The pursuit of growth opportunities. • Observance of the highest standards of corporate governance
Hanson (1994 Report)	Hanson is a diversified industrial management company with major investments in basic industries, including coal, chemicals, propane, building materials, forest products, tobacco and material handling. Our well established brand names enjoy leading market positions. Employing 74,000 people worldwide, our operating subsidiaries are principally located in the UK and the USA. [...] Our objective is to enhance shareholder value by increasing earnings per share and dividends as a result of internal growth and selective acquisitions. This has been achieved over the past thirty years by combining profitable investment with dedicated in-depth management who have profit-based incentives to produce the maximum long-term return on the capital for which they are accountable.

4.2.1   The meaning of profitability

Although we said earlier that concentrating on the economic welfare of shareholders and owners simplifies the task of setting objectives, the organisation is faced with the separate problem of what measure to use in maximising these benefits. The main options are:

- *Profits or accounting return* – This may seem straightforward, but raises questions of what the measure of profitability should be: reported profits, profitability as a percentage of sales revenue, return on assets employed, return on equity, etc. The investment recovery period and the estimated risk attached to invested capital should also be reflected in the return rate.

- *Cash returns* – Recognising some of the idiosyncratic problems of accounting measures of profitability, we can measure economic welfare by expected future net cash flows. These will usually be discounted for relative risk and the time value of money represented in the cost of capital, through techniques such as the Internal Rate of Return or Net Present Value.

- *Economic profits and rent* – Starting from the proposition that there is an expected 'normal' rate of return on assets, from capital invested in a market for any particular industry, 'rents' in excess of these 'profits' only accrue where an organisation exploits a competitive advantage. A measure of strategic success could therefore be the earning of economic rents.

Profits and accounting return are probably the most widely used measures of value flows, but it is widely accepted that cash return and economic profits and rent are more meaningful measures of economic benefit. This course certainly promotes the view that gaining and sustaining competitive advantage is a central concern for strategists. It follows that the pursuit of economic rents is a primary objective for organisations.

You should also note that the Set Book accompanying this course takes the view that businesses pursue a primary organisational objective of maximising profit. You will be familiar with many of the arguments in favour of this approach from your earlier studies.

Activity 4.1

To refresh your earlier studies, you should now read the sections in the Set Book entitled 'Strategy as a quest for profit' and 'Practical issues in linking value-based management to strategy' in Chapter 2 (pp. 32–45). In particular, if you feel uncertain as to the principles that lie behind the discounted cash flow approaches to valuing organisations and shareholder value, it is essential that you revisit these techniques. In this case, ensure you understand the sub-sections in the Set Book entitled 'The shareholder value approach', 'Valuing companies and businesses', and 'Valuing strategies' (pp. 36–39).

You should now attempt to state clearly, and briefly, what is meant by:

- the ambiguity of profit maximisation
- the difference between economic profit and accounting profit
- economic rent
- the concept of 'Economic Value Added' (EVA) and how this type of profit measure may increase the efficiency of a business
- the relationship between EVA and the maximisation of shareholder value
- the differences in stock market valuations using price-earnings ratios and net present values
- how cash flows can forecast in NPV calculations
- the purpose of valuing alternative strategies
- the problems of valuing alternative strategies, including strategy options
- advantages and disadvantages of short-term profit-maximisation as a strategic objective
- how accounting rates of return and 'balanced scorecards' can help managers monitor and control performance.

Discussion

As a result of this activity you should now be able to explain why the 'measure of profit used is less important than recognising the limitations and biases inherent in the measure used' (Chapter 2, p. 41). It is as well, also, to remember that the overall purpose of such measures of profitability (and general returns on investments) is to allow the organisation to take strategic decisions consistent with building positions of sustainable advantage for the long term and the most efficient use of resources to enable it to do so. That is what Grant means when he argues that 'most strategies involve a stream of resource-allocation decisions over time' (Chapter 2, p. 40).

Reflection _____

Consider now which profitability and/or performance measures are used in your own organisation.

_____

4.2.2   Shareholder value and share price

For most commercial organisations the pursuit of overall profitability, as a measure of the economic value added, will normally be a primary objective. This is not the same, however, as pursuing the maximisation of a quoted share value. There are a number of reasons why share value does not directly represent the underlying value added by the company itself:

- On most market trading days a share price is the market's valuation of the worth of the marginal amount of shares traded in a company that day – no more than a few per cent of total equity at most. A small package of shares does not usually confer control over the operations of the company. This is one reason why share values often rise when takeover bids are announced: a potential bidder is likely to recognise the additional value of controlling the activities and underlying cash flows of the company.

- Markets may value the combined worth of a diversified conglomerate at a discount to the underlying value of the separate activities. This has been a problem for conglomerates such as General Motors (which demerged EDS), ICI (which demerged its pharmaceutical activities as a separate entity, Zeneca), or Hanson (which demerged its various activities in 1996). A shareholder here would benefit from gaining access to the value of the demerged underlying activities, rather than simply selling a share in the conglomerate.

- Markets are subject to all sorts of imperfections in the way they operate, primarily concerning differentials in the information available to different investors. Only certain information must be legally disclosed, and analysts spend considerable time trying to obtain unique insights to underlying activities, or the intentions of other investors on the market. This can lead to relative over- and under-valuations of shares. Spotting imperfections and mis-valuations is at the heart of investment speculation, arbitrage, and market-making.

4.3   MANAGING STAKEHOLDER OBJECTIVES – NON-SHAREHOLDER OWNERSHIP AND TRUST RELATIONSHIPS

One of the problems encountered when dealing with the model of strategy that emphasises shareholder objectives is how to deal with the large number of organisations where ownership and the right to residual benefits cannot be easily determined in this way. The most notable organisations that do not fit this model are public-sector, charitable and trust-based organisations.

In all these organisations, there is usually a significant purpose of trust (or 'benefit for others') either explicitly made in purpose statements or implicit in their relationships. Legally, public sector and charitable organisations exist to fulfil the wishes of donors and funding agents in respect of some designated purpose or activity. The return to the providers of resources is the fulfilment of their wishes, rather than an economic reward such as a shareholders' dividend. Primary purposes and objectives for such organisations might therefore be:

- The implementation of social or public policy, such as the provision of health care or law and order, the regulation of monopolistic trading, or the equitable and efficient collection of taxation receipts.

- The completion of some charitable purpose, such as the promotion of natural childbirth, or the development of appropriate technology for farming in Tanzania.

These seem fairly obvious explicit purposes for charities and public-sector organisations, but managers in such organisations must be alert to the implicit wishes of donors and resource providers when establishing such trusts:

- A senior manager in a health department or a quasi-autonomous regulatory body would be naive not to recognise that politicians who set public and social policy have political purposes.

- The directors of charities must recognise that, for many donors, relief of conscience and contributing to a common cause are important outcomes. Thus, reporting the results of charitable activity may be as important to fulfilling donors' wishes as undertaking the activity itself.

In considering such organisations, however, it is also important to emphasise the essential similarities with 'commercial' organisations: the organisation must still secure scarce resources from providers, commit these to its activities, and ensure an adequate return (the fulfilment of wishes) to the resource providers.

There are, of course, difficulties encountered using quantifiable value measures in the public and charitable sectors. Attempts to introduce economic measures have often depended on the creation of internal quasi-markets by disaggregating the roles of service purchasers and providers, such as has happened in the UK's National Health Service. Alternatively, they have sometimes focused on performance measures other than profit-oriented ones:

- *Cost–benefit analysis* – The benefits from public services are often intangible in nature. In the 1960s and 1970s, techniques such as cost–benefit analysis were developed to try to quantify the positive and negative effects of such services for society at large. This was a popular technique in transport policy, for example, in comparing the social cost of trains versus automobiles.

- *Efficiency and effectiveness* – Recognising that a political or policy decision to provide a service may have already been taken, the objective of a public-service provider unit may be focused on efficient cost provision or the effectiveness of the service provided.

The opportunity cost of the provision of public and charitable services should also be recognised. It may be helpful, therefore, to consider the alternative uses of resources that funders have. In developed or industrialised countries such as France, Sweden, Ireland, Italy, the Netherlands and the USA, the issue of whether current levels of public services funding can be sustained in the long term has increasingly come into question. Often the demand for services seems to have no natural limit (as has been argued in the case of health services). In these circumstances, there is a choice to be made as to whether taxes should be raised to fund services, or to allow individuals to spend or invest their income. If the decision is taken to raise taxes, there is a further choice to make between which public services or investments to support. This argument suggests that in public services some kind of 'return on funding' measure which recognises opportunity cost would be desirable. Whether such a measure could be easily or meaningfully calculated is more problematic.

Reflection _____

What kind of purposes and objectives do you feel could be best applied to public services?

Can the requirements of social and public policy be easily reconciled with the creation of internal markets, cost–benefit approaches, or demands for efficiency and effectiveness?

If economic values are applied to (say) health service provision, what kind of measures could be used to evaluate these?

_____

The justification that a market makes more efficient allocation of resources is sometimes used to support the abandonment of public supply of services. In the USA it has been widely believed by libertarians that less government is better government, and that individuals are entitled to spend their income as they choose. Collective responsibility for social welfare needs is more widely accepted in Europe, although recent experience suggests European governments are encouraging individual responsibilities for social welfare.

Recent years have also seen the privatisation of many services previously supplied through public-sector organisations – and a growth in publicly funded charities taking over many of these responsibilities. Such privatisations range from changes in disability allowances which encourage private permanent health insurance cover in the UK, through attempts by the French and Italian governments to limit state exposure to large pension liabilities, to the opening up of the German national telephone monopoly.

4.4 MANAGING MANAGERS' OBJECTIVES

4.4.1 The manager's conflict of interest and the problem of 'agency'

One of the outcomes of the growth of commercial concerns in the nineteenth century was a move from owner-managed concerns to those where managers were in effective control of businesses, and profits were remitted to owners through dividends. This created an 'agency' relationship where the manager acted as *agent* for the principal, or owner. As with most agency relationships, a potential conflict of interest (sometimes described as 'moral hazard') arises (Jensen and Meckling, 1976). Managers, legally charged with accounting for profits to the owners, may use the discretion of control of assets for their own benefit.

4.4.2 The manager's interest

The purposes and objectives of managers have been considered by a number of writers:

- Baumol (1966) suggested that managers were interested in the *prestige* associated with *high market share* in their industry.

- Marris (1964) thought that managers were interested in *power* and *personal reward*, and that this showed in attempts to *grow* the asset base of the business (e.g. by acquisitions).

- Williamson (1974) believed that managers are primarily concerned with *status* and *empire-building*, increasing *salary*, and receiving *perks*.

- Galbraith (1967) studied the role of specialist managers in large firms. These he termed the 'technostructure', and believed they were interested in *growth*, managerial *independence* and *challenge* (e.g. through innovation).

The manager as agent – an illustration from *Dombey and Son* (Charles Dickens, 1848). The character of Mr. Carker is the first appearance in fiction of someone described as a manager. 'Between Mr. Dombey and the common world, as it was accessible through the medium of the outer office ... there were two degrees of descent. Mr Carker in his own office was the first step; Mr. Morfin, in *his* own office, was the second. Each of these gentlemen occupied a little chamber like a bath-room, opening from the passage outside Mr. Dombey's door. Mr. Carker, as Grand Vizier, inhabited the room that was nearest to the Sultan. Mr. Morfin, as an officer of inferior state, inhabited the room that was nearest to the clerks.'

These managerial objectives will be familiar to you in the context of private-sector employment. Managers in the public sector also pursue objectives that recognise career and political aims, and emphasise efficiency in managerial tasks. While the 'purposes' of the UK's Department of Health in Section 3.5 suggest the maximisation of health care benefits to the populace, the purposes of the UK's Department of Social Security seem to focus more on key political relationships with government ministers and the fulfilment of managerial obligations:

1 To support [government] ministers in the development and implementation of social security policy.

2 To pay social security benefits.

3 To arrange for the collection of National Insurance Contribution [a form of taxation].

4 To carry out other services in accordance with the law.
    (Department of Social Security, 1993 Report)

Theories concerning the interests of managers tend to imply that owners cannot trust managers. Indeed, it has been suggested that these views represent a 'theory of management delinquency' (Donaldson, 1995, p. 166). You may or may not agree with this view, but it would be naive not to recognise the potential conflict of interest.

Reflection _____

Consider the organisation you work for, or one that you are familiar with. Do you recognise objectives being set that serve managerial interests? Do these accord with the ideas of Baumol, Marris, Williamson and Galbraith listed above? Finally, consider whether you think these managerial interests conflict directly with the interests of owners or other stakeholders.

4.4.3 Aligning ownership and managerial interests

Most of the managerial objectives noted in Section 4.4.2 are not necessarily in direct conflict with an objective of maximising profits or added value to shareholders. Where conflict is likely, however, a number of approaches can help align the interests of owners and managers:

* Increased monitoring of management by owners through, for example, audit procedures, independent non-executive directors, and director remuneration committees.

* Incentives for management to identify with owner objectives, including profit-related bonuses, or share options.

* Sanctions or threat of sanctions for poor performance. Thus, offering short fixed-term contracts reduces the security that incumbent directors feel.

* The provision of clear audited information to owners and capital markets to allow them to make their judgements on management performance.

* Capital and finance markets that encourage takeovers. This allows investors to replace poor management with ease, and creates a market for 'corporate control' of assets.

Many of these measures can also be applied by large or diversified companies to help align the interests of the management of business units or divisions. This approach can be seen in the operations of Hanson, as suggested in its profile shown in Table 4.1. On the other hand, mechanisms to overcome the hazards of managerial agency and conflicts of interest may be much harder to implement in public and charitable sector organisations for the very reason that measures of performance are more difficult to establish and operationalise.

Example: Berkshire Hathaway

Some managers make a virtue out of emphasising the interests of owners as paramount. Berkshire Hathaway owns an insurance company, operates a 'Savings and Loan', publishes the *Buffalo News* and an encyclopaedia, manufactures workplace uniforms, dry-cleaning systems and chocolate candies, and retails home furnishings and jewellery. As it has grown it has also acquired substantial stakes in large companies such as Salomon Brothers and US Air. A business that has had a very loyal investor base, it is headed by Warren E. Buffett, whose influence is obvious:

> With so many new shareholders, it's appropriate to summarize the major business principles we follow that pertain to the manager-owner relationship:

- Although our form is corporate, our attitude is partnership. Charlie Munger and I think of our shareholders as owner-partners, and of ourselves as managing partners ... We do not view the company itself as the ultimate owner of our business assets but, instead, view the company as a conduit through which our shareholders own the assets.

- In line with this owner-orientation, our directors are major shareholders of Berkshire Hathaway. In the case of at least four, over 50% of family net worth is represented by holdings of Berkshire. We eat our own cooking.

- Our long-term economic goal (subject to some qualifications mentioned later) is to maximize the average annual rate of gain of intrinsic business value on a per-share basis. We do not measure the economic significance or performance of Berkshire by its size; we measure per-share progress.

- [...] because of the limitations of conventional accounting, consolidated reported earnings may reveal relatively little about our true economic performance. Charlie and I, both as owners and managers, virtually ignore such consolidated numbers. However, we will also report to you the earnings of each major business we control, numbers we consider of great importance. These figures, along with other information we will supply about the individual businesses, should generally aid you in making judgements about them.

- [...] We will reject interesting opportunities rather than over-leverage our balance sheet. This conservatism has penalized our results but it is the only behavior that leaves us comfortable, considering our fiduciary obligations to policyholders, depositors, lenders and the many equity holders who have committed unusually large portions of their net worth to our care. (As one of the Indianapolis '500' winners said: 'To finish first, you must first finish.')

- A managerial 'wish list' will not be filled at shareholder expense. We will not diversify by purchasing entire businesses at prices that ignore long-term economic consequences to our shareholders. We will only do with your money what we would do with our own, weighing fully the values you can obtain by diversifying your own portfolios through direct purchases in the stock market.

- You should be fully aware of one attitude Charlie and I share that hurts our financial performance: regardless of price, we have no interest at all in selling any good businesses that Berkshire owns, and are very reluctant to sell sub-par businesses as long as we expect them to generate at least some cash ... We hope not to repeat the capital-allocation mistakes that led us into such sub-par businesses ... [but] gin rummy managerial behaviour (discard your least promising business at each turn) is not our style. [...]

- We will be candid in our reporting to you, emphasizing the pluses and minuses important in appraising business value. Our guideline is to tell you the business facts that we would want to know if our positions were reversed. [...]

- Despite our policy of candour we will discuss our activities in marketable securities only to the extent legally required. Good investment ideas are rare, valuable and subject to competitive appropriation just as good product or business acquisition ideas are. Therefore, we normally will not talk about our investment ideas.

  (Warren E. Buffett, Berkshire Hathaway Report, 1989)

Activity 4.2 _____

Berkshire Hathaway clearly give the interests of shareholders pre-eminence when setting company objectives. You should now list the ideas for aligning managerial and owner interest and objectives from Section 4.4.3 that are prominent in Berkshire Hathaway's statement. Consider also those areas of its investment policy that deviate from the specified long-term economic goal of value growth on a per-share basis. What is the likely attitude of shareholders in Berkshire to these deviations?

4.5 STAKEHOLDERS AS COLLABORATORS

There is a growing view that corporate responsibility means that an organisation needs to manage the strategic contribution of resources by, and payment of rewards to, all stakeholders. This is not born out of a view that inclusive collective approaches are in any way ethically superior to those which stress the dominance of shareholders or owners. The organisation may simply have more chance of achieving long-term success (however defined) by facing the need to manage all important relationships strategically.

There are a number of reasons that can be advanced for this challenge to the orthodox belief that shareholder and owner interests should be given overriding primacy in setting an organisation's purposes and objectives:

- The increasing importance in business of intangible rather than physical assets makes owners of shares – providers of financial capital – potentially subservient to the owners of such intangible resources. For example, an information systems company must give due regard to the wishes of key software developers. Equally, market-makers in investments often depend on the insights of traders, analysts and researchers to give them a competitive edge in knowledge and information. The power that different stakeholders exert from the control of scarce resources (which we will discuss in Section 4.6.2) is ignored at the peril of the health of the organisation and, eventually, its owners.

- The market in 'corporate control', which suggests that ineffective managers can be removed through acquisition and takeover activity, is at best an imperfect, arbitrary and expensive mechanism. Imperfect because incumbent managers almost always have considerably more knowledge and information about the business than outsiders or existing shareholders. Expensive because the transaction costs of mounting a takeover bid are substantial – bankers, accountants, brokers, lawyers, and public relations consultants must all be paid. Finally, it is arbitrary from the viewpoint of the overall market, as there is no mechanism that guarantees that *all* inefficient companies become takeover targets.

- The need to attend to customer relationships as a driver in the enduring success of organisations should not be underestimated. A strategy that tried to increase shareholder returns at the expense of important aspects of customer value, such as reliability and specification levels, is unlikely to increase shareholder returns over the long term. Indeed such a strategy will destroy ultimate shareholder value. Customers are usually a key provider of financial resources for an organisation.

The interests of shareholders and owners are, ultimately, probably best served by an acceptance of the need for stakeholder management. For example, Kay (1993) and Baden-Fuller and Stopford (1996) point out that attending to shareholder and stakeholder interests are not mutually exclusive. By definition, an organisation is a collaboration of interested parties, and is therefore unlikely to be a 'zero-sum' game where the only way that one party can benefit (e.g. a shareholder) is at the expense of another (e.g. employees or management). 'Non-zero-sum' games are those where additional wealth or benefit is created through the process of collaboration. This is the difference between seeing an organisation as a mere set of competing financial claims and recognising it as a network of long-term relationships. Baden-Fuller and Stopford suggest that the importance of the stakeholder approach is that, metaphorically, it allows management to concentrate on making a bigger cake, rather than concentrating too much on how the existing cake is cut up and shared out.

4.5.1 Using contract theory to analyse stakeholder collaboration

It is worth while finding a way to analyse what keeps the parties together in stakeholder relationships, making sure their best interests are served. Kay (1993) categorises relationships by identifying three different types of 'contracts' (spot, classical and relational), which might govern the relationships of stakeholders:

1 *Spot contracts* – 'I sell, you buy, and that is that. We might, or might not, engage in a similar contract next week, or next year. Spot contracts are easy to make and cheap to transact. Spot contracts do not need lengthy negotiation. Nor are expensive lawyers called to draft their provisions. Spot contracts are based on standard terms and take place at market prices. We make so many spot contracts that we often hardly think of them as contracts at all, and the law infers a contractual intention from our behaviour ... Spot contracts are effective when individually selfish behaviour works to the best joint interest of the parties.' (Kay, pp. 50–51). Examples of spot contracts include the purchase of commodity supplies, or hiring a taxi.

Kay continues, 'although spot contracts form a majority – by number – of business relationships, the most important of commercial relationships are rarely spot contracts. Managers do not raise finance, rent property, hire senior employees, or deal with their principal suppliers through spot contracts.' (p. 51) Relationships with the most important of an organisation's stakeholders are unlikely, therefore, to be spot contracts, but will recognise the importance of co-operative behaviour. In saying this, we are not making a general statement that co-operative behaviour is always better than competitive or confrontational behaviour, we are simply saying that individual and collective stakeholder interests *within* an organisation are usually best served by recognising collaboration as an essence of long-term relationships.

What happens, then, when parties to a contract engage in similar transactions year after year, week in week out, day by day? What happens when 'individually selfish behaviour' does not work in the mutual joint interest of the contracting parties? There are two solutions to these problems, argues Kay, which best represent the nature of long-term stakeholder relationships:

2   *Classical contracts* – There are three strong reasons why stakeholders may seek to formalise a long-term relationship with another party (think of the legally explicit documentation that surrounds the ownership of a house or other property, and the mortgage finance secured on it). First, both sides must value the certainty that an extensive contract brings to their relationship. The knowledge that the terms of the contract (price, period of supply, extent of rights and obligations, etc.) will not be changed the following day – as they could on a spot market – must have value. Secondly, where switching costs would be incurred once a relationship has commenced, parties will seek to eliminate the likelihood that the relationship will be terminated. Finally, where a long-term relationship requires specific investments to be made that are dedicated to the relationship, the parties will seek to ensure that the relationship must continue, or that they are reimbursed for their investment. Examples of classical contracts include those for the long-term supply of customised parts and sub-assemblies, or the purchase of a lease on a property

3   *Relational contracts* – These contracts define many long-term relationships but are not characterised by the same degree of formality as classical contracts. In contrast to classical contracts, many of their terms are not written down but are implicit. Although there will normally be some legal agreement at the heart of a relational contract, the expectations of each party go well beyond these formal terms. At heart there is, rather, a trust relationship based on the understanding that mutual collaboration will deliver an increase in their joint wealth or welfare. It is important to an effective relational contract that each party recognises their dependence on each other in a series of repeated transactions over the long term. Examples of common relational contracts include contracts of employment, the supply of professional services, and marriage.

The difference between classical and relational contracts may be evidenced physically through the degree of formalisation of terms in the legal documentation. Differences of substance are, however, more important than these differences in legal documentation. There are three important differences of substance which will determine whether a relational or classical contract is more appropriate:

1   Both types are attempts to overcome some of the limitations of spot contracts by establishing long-term relationships. The classical contract does this by making explicit changes to the pay-off structure of the contract to bind the parties to co-operative long-term behaviours – there are rewards for collaboration and penalties for breaking the contract. Relational contracting is instead dependent on an implicit understanding that the parties must continue to co-operate in a series of repeated transactions for their mutual benefit.

2   Relational contracts suffer rather than benefit from precise specifications of terms and obligations. In relational contracts, the importance of a committed but flexible response to events is central to the success of the contract. Classical contracts, on the other hand, are best suited to long-term relationships that need absolute certainty of behaviour.

3   Flexibility is best achieved by free flows of information within a relational contract. On the contrary, there is no incentive for such a free flow of information in a classical contract (unless it is specifically covered by the contract itself as necessary to fulfil its obligations). Indeed, within the classical contract, information made available to another party might simply be used against you in due course when the contract is renewed.

Examples: mismatches in contract structures

In the UK and the USA in the late 1980s and 1990s there has been a move away from highly structured bargaining arrangements whereby unions and central managers determine very precise, highly specified employment practice, reward and remuneration policies. 'Working to rule' is increasingly seen as a luxury which neither employers nor employees can afford. Associated outsourcing of work (often to former employees) can be seen either as an attempt to turn employment into a spot market, or, perhaps more realistically if such transactions are repeated, as a shift towards more flexible long-term arrangements based around relational contracting.

A further example of contract structure mismatch became evident in 1996 when British Gas disclosed substantial liabilities in respect of 'take-or-pay' obligations with producers of North Sea natural gas. These contracts largely derived from an earlier period of market regulation when the development of gas fields was legally dependent on a highly specified supply agreement being in force to cover the projected life of the field (up to 25 years). Even after initial deregulation, however, British Gas continued to write more of these contracts. By 1995, the legislation to complete the deregulation of the UK gas market by 1998 was largely in place and the commoditised nature of the market for gas supply reasserted itself. These long-term classical contracts which required British Gas to buy specified volumes of gas at above-market prices were conservatively estimated to lead to likely losses of £1.5 billion. The economic structure of the market after deregulation had shifted to favour spot contracting for commodity natural gas in the short term, and more flexible relational contracting for the long term.

Activity 4.3

Returning to the organisation you work for, or one you are familiar with, analyse the major stakeholder relationships using Kay's classification of contracts. Which are spot, classical, and relational contracts? After you have done this, consider whether, in your opinion, any of these relationships would best serve the organisation and its stakeholders if it was restructured as another type of contract. Is there a mismatch between the actual and optimal relationship structure with stakeholders?

Discussion _____

For example, your organisation might be used to sourcing industry-standard parts from a variety of suppliers, all making identical components. Traditional practice has often meant that these supplier relationships were governed by spot contracting. You may, however, believe that the reliability and quality of these parts is becoming more important for your own organisation's product. In these circumstances, it may become more appropriate to develop relational contracts with a limited number of suppliers, where suppliers and customer work flexibly towards building better quality over the long term. This type of change in supplier relationships has led car manufacturers such as Volkswagen, Peugeot, Ford and General Motors to reduce the number of component suppliers dramatically – sometimes from 200 or 300 to 15 or 20.

4.6   IMPORTANT DIMENSIONS OF A STAKEHOLDER ANALYSIS

4.6.1   Returns on resources and rewards for stakeholders

All stakeholders, in contributing resources to an organisation, will seek a return. The organisation must, therefore, utilise these resources to provide that return. As you should now be aware, stakeholders have many different reasons for participating in an organisation, and the returns they require are not necessarily economic or financial in nature. We will borrow from economics, however, to consider the implications of achieving different rates of return.

Returns to stakeholders are inextricably linked over the long run to the returns an organisation makes and its ability to finance attractive rewards to resource contributors. Resources on which a return might be expected include finance, labour, knowledge and information, political backing, raw materials or component parts, or access to a distribution channel. Returns might be denominated in financial value, political favours, fulfilment of personal objectives, etc.

Wherever there is a *perfect market* for resources there will be an expectation that those resources will earn a *'normal' rate of return*. A perfect market is characterised by the inability of any competitors to gain any kind of advantage. In this type of market competitors will receive an identical average rate of return on their resources, and their objective must be to match their competitors' efficiency and effectiveness – if not, the organisational stakeholders and resource contributors will simply switch allegiance to a competitor.

If an organisation makes *above-average rates of return* on their resources relative to other organisations in their sector, this must indicate some kind of competitive advantage over their competitors. Either the market for the use of their particular resources and capabilities will be *imperfect* or an individual organisation will have a *distinctive* or *unique advantage*. Making above-average rates of return on resources means that stakeholder rewards can be enhanced, making it easier to continue to attract necessary resources, in a virtuous circle.

If an organisation makes *below-average rates of return*, it will eventually lose the ability to supply stakeholders with adequate rewards and, thus, their support. For example, a brewery quoted on a stock market consistently achieves smaller returns than its competitors who have worked hard to drive process efficiencies in their breweries. Investors who want to invest in brewing will be attracted to sell its shares and reinvest in its competitors. This will tend to drive down the price of the shares in the inefficient company, and make the cost of acquiring equity finance relatively more expensive for it. Normally, the minimum objective of such an organisation will be to turn around its performance to at least normal rates of return.

Book 1 stated: 'This course is about those actions that determine whether an organisation survives, prospers, or dies.' Organisational survival, prosperity and death can, in normal circumstances, be associated with a persistent ability of the organisation to make normal, above-average, or below-average rates of return, respectively. The pursuit of competitive advantage and above-average rates of return are assumed to be important overriding objectives for organisations of all types. This is regardless of whether the measure of return is financial, political, or emotional.

4.6.2   Competition for scarce resources

The above assumption is dependent on another: that most organisations face a limit on the availability of certain key resources. They are therefore forced to make decisions about their use that carry opportunity costs and benefits. Most organisations are forced, therefore, to deal with the process of *competition* both to acquire scarce resources and for opportunities to use these resources and earn an above-average return for stakeholders.

This is an important idea because it is self-evident that where resources are freely available there is no need for organisations to compete for them. The costs of acquiring freely available resources are only the costs of locating, transporting, and using them. It is where supplies of resources are limited that competition becomes important.

Example: competing for water

Despite occasional progress in resolving the conflict between Israel and its neighbours in the Middle East, geopolitical commentators express continuing concern for the stability of the region. A fundamental concern is the potential for conflict over access to the limited supplies of water available.

The region is served by a limited number of waterways (the Euphrates, the Jordan) which generally flow to the sea through a number of nations. In addition, there are natural underground water flows between, for example, Syria, Iraq, Saudi Arabia and Jordan. Already there are significant disparities between per capita water supplies available, with Israel and, particularly, Jordan having extremely poor resources. Water is relatively scarce in all these countries and schemes to improve supplies in 'upstream' countries such as Iraq and Syria lead to accusations from 'downstream' countries, such as Israel and Jordan, that the 'natural' flow rates of the River Jordan available to them are being reduced. Attempts to manage this potential area of conflict and recognise the shared nature of the resource give rise to treaties (classical contracts) which specify volumes of water available to each party and restrictions on usage.

The scarcity and importance of water as a resource in the region can also be seen through the construction of extremely costly water desalination plants in Saudi Arabia and the United Arab Emirates, funded by the tax revenues from the far more abundant supplies of crude oil.

4.6.3 Sources of stakeholder power

The control of scarce resources goes to the heart of an effective stakeholder analysis, but there are many other sources of power in an organisation. We will consider the significance of power in organisations in Books 6 and 8. To identify the best structure for the relationships and contracts between stakeholders, however, it is important to be realistic about the balance of power between them. For now, therefore, consider how the twelve sources of power identified by Morgan (1986) might affect a stakeholder analysis intended to determine the objectives of an organisation:

1   *Formal authority* – Power deriving from a formal position (in management or as a director) and recognised as legitimate by others in the organisation.

2   *Control of scarce resources* – Those who own or have access to particular scarce resources have power relative to those who need those resources.

3   *Organisational structures and procedures* – Formal systems and structures can be manipulated to favour one group of managers over another, for example regional sales managers may have prominence over head office functional specialists.

4   *Control of decision processes* – The ability to influence the context or framing of decision-making can confer power on owners, managers, government agencies, regulators, unions, or employees.

5   *Control of knowledge and information* – Even in unsophisticated businesses a clear knowledge and understanding of exactly how the business works and can be controlled, confers power and influence. Knowledge and information are themselves becoming important products and services for businesses, explicitly recognising their value.

6   *Boundary management* – The ability to monitor and control transactions with other parties outside the organisation is increasingly important as organisations 'outsource' more of their activities.

7   *Ability to manage uncertainty* – Uncertainty can be regarded as a potential problem impeding progress or preventing purposeful action. The ability to find solutions under conditions of uncertainty, or at least to find ways to start resolving problems, can be an important source of power.

8   *Control of technology* – The skilled process or craft of manipulating important technology may be an important source of power for groups of employees or suppliers. Alternatively, proprietary rights such as patents or licences over technology can enable suppliers to increase their returns.

9   *Alliances and informal networks* – Often based on mutual dependency and exchange, alliances and networks can provide groups of stakeholders with greater political influence. In addition, the

ability to use an alliance to, for example, obtain access to an important (otherwise unavailable) resource can increase an individual's influence.

10 *Countervailing power* – Countervailing power occurs when power tends to become concentrated in relatively few hands. In such situations, there is a tendency for those without such power to co-ordinate their actions in opposition and to gain legitimacy from the status of opposition. This can be seen in parliamentary democracies, but might also be considered as the original basis for the growth of trade unions.

11 *Symbolism and the management of meaning* – If managers are to influence employees, suppliers, customers, government and owners, they must learn to manage the messages and meanings that are conveyed by their actions. This is at the heart of, for example, brand advertising, but may also be crucial in implementing a change in employee behaviours.

12 *Gender power* – Power may often accrue to groups or individuals based on assumed stereotypes of gender roles. This analysis could also be extended to describe differences in relative power positions in multi-racial organisations.

Activity 4.4

Construct a stakeholder diagram and analysis for key groups in an organisation with which you are familiar. For each stakeholder relationship identify:

1   the nature of the resource contributed
2   the relative scarcity of that resource
3   the nature of the return or reward received by that stakeholder
4   whether that stakeholder is able to accrue normal, above-average, or below-average rates of return on the resources they contribute
5   whether there are any other sources of power that those stakeholders are able to exert.

Finally, consider the significance of the influence of individual stakeholder groups in helping to frame the purposes and objectives of the organisation. If possible, rank the relative importance of stakeholders in determining the organisation's objectives.

4.7 IMPLICATIONS OF ADOPTING A STAKEHOLDER PERSPECTIVE

Treating strategy as the management of key resources and organisational relationships, as the stakeholder approach implies, leads to specific consequences for the organisation. Decisions about products, markets or activities are still important, reflecting the importance of resources flowing into and out of operations. Structures, systems and processes must still be managed. In addition, however, strategic concerns flow from relationships with stakeholders, and include:

• the need to balance the *objectives* of different stakeholders
• the objective of producing normal or above-average *rates of return* for stakeholders

- the *politics* of handling the relative power and influence of scarce resource contributors
- the management of *culture and meaning* between and with stakeholders.

5 SUMMARY AND CONCLUSION

This book has been concerned with the identification of the role of organisational purposes and objectives in strategy. In Section 1 we considered whether the organisation is a separate entity or construct, or whether the organisation seems no more than an aggregation of individuals. We also set out certain assumptions:

> ... organisations are collaborative devices with common collective purposes which are not necessarily identical to the purposes of individual members of the organisation. For individuals to remain members, however, there must be an acceptable alignment of individual and collective purposes and objectives, values and beliefs, and sense of identity.

The focus on 'purpose statements' rather than just on 'missions' or 'visions' indicates that, to understand an organisation's actions better, we should identify its underlying values, beliefs and identity. In this, such statements can provide a link with an organisation's past, indicating issues that mattered in its history, and perhaps identifying the capabilities and resources on which the organisation's success is built and may depend in the future. The language of purpose statements can be very important in this, if we are to grasp the meaning that lies behind them, or the assumptions on which they are built. Indeed, purposes, values and beliefs can be as easily conveyed in routine organisational documents, when they are thoroughly understood and underpin the daily actions of the organisation. Witness again the magazine advertisement for L.L. Bean quoted in Section 3.3:

> The Golden Rule of L.L. Bean: sell good merchandise at a reasonable profit, treat your customers like human beings, and they'll always come back for more.

An effective purpose statement can therefore convey an important sense of collective identity for the organisation and its members, and help to create a consensus for action amongst its many stakeholders.

All stakeholders bring resources or capabilities as their part of collaboration in an organisation. In turn, they expect a personal reward (however this is defined). Exactly what reward they achieve, and what influence they have over a collective statement of values or purposes, can be determined only by analysing the nature of their relative power and the basis of the long-term contractual relationships that govern their participation in the organisation. Ultimately, however, an effective sense of collective organisational purpose will be achieved only where collective interests are reasonably aligned with individual purposes. Managing stakeholder relationships lies at the heart of establishing a coherent sense of organisational purpose.

REFERENCES

Baden-Fuller, C. and Stopford, J.M. (1996) *Rejuvenating the Mature Business*, Routledge, London.

Baumol, W.J. (1966) *Business Behaviour, Value and Growth*, Harcourt Brace, New York.

David, F.R. (1989) 'How companies define their mission', *Long Range Planning*, Vol. 22, No. 1.

Donaldson, L. (1995) *American Anti-Management Theories of Organisation*, Cambridge University Press, Cambridge.

Eccles, R.G. and Nohria, N. (1992) *Beyond the Hype: rediscovering the essence of management*, Harvard Business School Press, Boston, MA.

Etzioni, A. (1971) *A Comparative Analysis of Complex Organisations*, The Free Press, New York.

Galbraith, J.K. (1967) *The New Industrial State*, Hamish Hamilton, London.

Grant, R.M. (1998) *Contemporary Strategy Analysis* (3rd edn), Blackwell, Oxford (the Set Book).

Jensen, M.C. and Meckling, W.H. (1976) 'Theory of the firm: managerial behaviour, agency costs and ownership structure', *Journal of Financial Economics*, Vol. 3, pp. 305–360.

Kay, J. (1993) *Foundations of Corporate Success*, Oxford University Press, Oxford.

Marris, R.L. (1964) *The Economic Theory of 'Managerial' Capitalism*, Macmillan, London.

Morgan, G. (1986) *Images of Organisation*, Sage, Newbury Park, CA.

Pearce, J.A. (1982) 'The company mission as a strategic tool', *Sloan Management Review*, Spring, pp. 15–24.

Thornton, D.W. (1995) *Airbus Industrie: the politics of an international industrial collaboration*, St. Martin's Press, New York.

Williamson, O.E. (1974) *The Economics of Discretionary Behaviour: managerial objectives in a theory of the firm*, Kershaw, London.

ACKNOWLEDGEMENTS

Grateful acknowledgement is made to the following sources for permission to reproduce material in this book:

Text

Pages 32–33: Buffett, W. E. 1990, Berkshire Hathaway Inc. Annual Report 1989, Berkshire Hathaway Inc. Reprinted with permission.

Illustrations

Page 15: Bara-King Photographic Inc.; *Page 30: Dealings with the Firm of Dombey and Son, Wholesale, Retail, and for Exportation,* London, Oxford University Press, 1950.

BOOK 3

ANALYSING EXTERNAL RELATIONSHIPS

Prepared by David Asch, Harold Carter and Susan Segal-Horn
for the B820 Course Team

CONTENTS

1 INTRODUCTION

This book is designed to develop your understanding of the environment in which your organisation operates. The focus is on the 'near' environment – the structure of the industry, strategic groups and the competitive context of the organisation. Later parts of the course will broaden the scope of your understanding of the rich mix of issues which influence the strategies of organisations.

Understanding the external environment in order to develop a competitive strategy that the organisation is capable of delivering is crucial to the organisation's success. The complexity of the competitive arena should not be underestimated. You should recall the drivers for change in the 'competitive milieu' proposed by Prahalad and Hamel, reported in Book 1. Stopford and Baden-Fuller (1990) conducted extensive research amongst European firms and noted that in mature industries: 'Behind the veneer of stability, represented by static or only slowly shifting total demand, lie complex, deep-seated and continuous processes of change.'

We focus on how such continuous external change affects the profitability and performance of organisations. Both commercial and not-for-profit organisations can and do compete in an environment for key resources which can form the bases of sources of competitive or strategic advantage.

To study this book you need:
- Case Study Book
- Set Book
- Video Cassette 1

1.1 LEARNING OBJECTIVES OF THIS BOOK

After studying this book, you should be able to:

- demonstrate the importance of the business environment in influencing organisational strategy
- use analytical tools and models to help your understanding of different forces at work in the environment
- identify key issues in the external environment, distinguishing them from the many other external forces which will have a lesser impact on your organisation
- propose appropriate organisational responses to environmental change and changes in industry structures
- start to analyse the patterns of interaction between competitors and the routes by which they pursue competitive advantage.

These objectives underpin the structure of the remainder of this book. The book starts with a very broad 'macro' picture of the environment (Section 2) and then moves from a wider to a narrower focus as it progresses from developing understanding of an industry, to a strategic group, to competing organisations. Section 3 introduces industry structures and asks the question: 'Why do most organisations in some industries compete in very different ways from most organisations in some other industries?' Section 4 introduces the concept of strategic groups *within* an industry. The ideas of strategic space and industry dynamics are then considered. The emphasis here is on understanding how industries and organisations evolve over time. Section 5 considers the key success factors within the processes of organisations, and how we can systematically analyse the differences between organisations within an industry or group. Section 6 looks briefly at the forces which underpin the emergence of co-operative or competitive strategies in a sector, and which shape the ways in which organisations interact with one another.

In each section the concepts covered will be used to analyse a real situation, and make recommendations. Sections 3 and 5 will make use of the Electrolux case study, which you will find in the Case Study Book, as the basis for this activity. Section 4 will use research on the European food-processing industry.

2 THE FAR AND NEAR ENVIRONMENTS

In order to commence our exploration of the environments in which organisations operate we should first examine the concept of the 'business environment'. The term is used in a variety of ways: for example, to refer to the prevailing economic conditions of a country within which a business operates. In other instances it is used to describe the totality of conditions in which an organisation operates. 'Business environment' is also used interchangeably with the term 'competitive environment', that is any situation which impacts on the competitive capability of a business organisation. These different interpretations might, at first glance, appear somewhat confusing. However, each interpretation of the term is valid.

Kotler (1980) identified four levels of the environment which surround an organisation:

1 The *task environment*, which consists of the major participants in the performance of the organisation's task, such as suppliers, distributors and final buyers.

2 The *competitive environment*, which consists of organisations which compete with the organisation for customers and scarce resources of all types.

3 The *public environment*, which consists of institutions which watch or regulate the activities of the organisation or the sector in which it is located.

4 The *macro-environment*, which consists of the major societal forces which confront the organisation, i.e. demography, economics, natural resources, technology, politics and culture.

2.1 WHAT CONSTITUTES THE FAR ENVIRONMENT?

We include in the far environment Kotler's public environment and macro-environment. Later in the course we will consider the issue of the organisation's interface with the public environment; here we will seek to remind you of key features in the macro-environment. Most of you will be familiar with the concept of STEP factors from your previous studies. You may recall that STEP factors are a major component of an organisation's external environment and comprise the following:

* Sociological factors, e.g. values, life styles, demographics
* Technological factors, e.g. research and development, new products and processes
* Economic factors, e.g. economic growth, inflation, interest rates
* Political factors, e.g. competitive policy, legislation, political parties.

Fahey and Narayanan's (1986, pp. 28–34) model of the macro-environment stresses that the environment can be understood only as a *system*, in which each factor is related to and affects every other factor (Figure 2.1). Their model offers a framework of analysis for identifying, tracking, projecting and assessing trends and patterns in the global macro-environment. It consists of four analytical stages:

1   scanning the environment to detect ongoing and emerging change

2   monitoring specific environmental trends and patterns to determine their evolution

3   forecasting the future direction of environmental changes

4   assessing current and future environmental changes for their strategic and organisational implications.

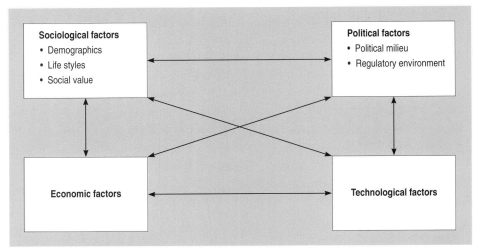

Figure 2.1   A model of the macro-environment (based on Fahey and Narayanan, 1986)

Fahey and Narayanan note the importance of going beyond mere description of change in the environment, to assessing the forces driving it. Forces driving change in one factor may often lie in changes in other factors. They note also that driving forces often interact and thus may reinforce one another, conflict and thus dampen one other, or be unrelated.

There are two important points to highlight at this stage: first, the list of factors that constitute an environment is almost endless; secondly, the list of relevant factors can vary from industry to industry and indeed from business to business; they are therefore context-specific.

2.2   WHAT CONSTITUTES A NEAR ENVIRONMENT?

Organisations can be thought of as sharing a near environment if they interact frequently with each other, or frequently affect the context in which others have to operate (Kotler's task and competitive environments). There are many ways in which others can influence all or part of an organisation's activities – for example by:

*   competing for its customers (either directly in terms of offering similar product benefits, or indirectly by competing for their expenditure); or by co-operating in helping to serve customers, via measures such as joint sales arrangements

*   acting as suppliers; or by competing for suppliers; or by establishing collaborative purchasing arrangements

- competing or collaborating in the pursuit of resources which are needed internally to enable the organisation to function – such as staff, land and sites, access to capital, research and development, technological know-how and so on
- competing or collaborating to capture and control elements of the external environment (for example, political support over issues such as land-use planning, industry standards, industrial policy, and so on).

Thus the near environment will seldom be made up of a single group of obvious 'competitors' – although experience suggests that it is often on such competitors that most management attention will focus. Rather, it can better be seen as a series of overlapping Venn diagrams, with many interacting combinations (see Figure 2.2).

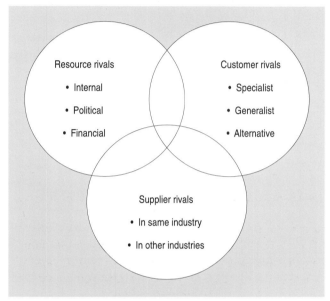

Figure 2.2   Influences on the near environment

All organisations will inevitably be involved in many such combinations of relationships. Each organisation will have its own distinctive set of interactions. Several organisations may agree on who are the 'direct' rivals – those in the middle of the Venn diagram – but the constituents of the outer parts of the circles will vary, organisation by organisation.

It can be extremely difficult, in practice, to focus organisational attention away from one's 'direct' rivals. Sometimes, however, these rivals do not have the greatest long-term potential for generating radical change in the nature of the near environment since they are likely to be constrained in similar ways. Thus the greatest changes may be brought about by those in the outer circles stepping over a barrier, using their existing technology or skills in new ways, to change key parts of the product or service offering; or disrupting, accidentally or deliberately, access to key resources.

The question of where attention needs to be focused in the near environment is partly one of timing. In the short term, the greatest possible impact may come from other organisations of a similar size which approach the product/service offering in a similar way. In the longer term, the greatest potential change could come from organisations with different capabilities or organisational profiles, to one's own.

3 INDUSTRY STRUCTURE

In seeking to construct a competitive strategy we need to understand what is likely to happen in the markets in which the organisation delivers its product and service. Since a market includes those consumers to whom an organisation can sell or deliver a product or service, the term is equally relevant to not-for-profit, as well as commercial, organisations. Other issues also need to be raised, in particular: 'What industry are we competing in?' In order to define the industry the organisation is in we must be clear about the needs of our customers and who it is that the organisation is competing with.

Defining the industry the organisation is in, and the competitors it is up against, is not necessarily a straightforward exercise. If mistakes are made in defining the market or industry, inappropriate strategies may be formulated. To define the industry the organisation is in currently, or indeed potentially, we must:

- identify buyers' needs
- define who our competitors are.

3.1 ANALYSING INDUSTRY STRUCTURE

When an acceptable definition of these industries has been established we can proceed to analyse systematically the competitive forces that are influencing them. Organisations rarely operate in just one, clearly defined, homogeneous industry. Most organisations, for example, operate in several markets, and within each market there are likely to be distinct segments of demand (segments being groups of buyers with similar needs).

 You should now read Chapter 3 of the Set Book, pages 51–83.

In reading this chapter you should pay particular attention to Grant's discussion of analysis of competition in an industry and to his description of Porter's 'five forces of competition' framework (Porter, 1980). Porter's approach concentrates on the competitive forces operating in the industry, the outcome being an assessment of the 'attractiveness' of the industry. Attractiveness is defined by how profitable the industry is for the firms already in it, relative to the average economic profits that might be expected to be made employing equivalent resources in a competitive market. (You may wish to recall the discussion of profit objectives in Book 2.)

Clearly the Porter framework is only one of several ways of analysing and understanding competition in a particular industry. Many managers find it a powerful model, because it corresponds with the operating environment in which most managers find themselves – having to deal with suppliers, serve customers, worry about potential competitors or new substitute products, and to jockey for position with other competing organisations. Not-for-profit managers may find the *buyer–supplier* axis particularly thought-provoking, regarding changing patterns of demand and/or new sources of supply.

We can examine each of the five forces for an overview of the scope the industry structure affords for the creation of added value for organisations within it. This can also give us a quick way of evaluating the likely impact of changes to the structure of the industry, since we can ask how those changes will be likely to impact on each of the five forces.

Although there are limitations on the use of Porter's framework, it can provide insights into the forces underlying competition in a particular industry. However, statements made on the basis of models of industry structure are likely to be helpful only for a limited time. When even one of the five forces changes its nature, this can destabilise the relationships of the other four. For example:

- Altered government regulation of the airline industry sharply reduced the barriers to entry for new airlines in the USA in the 1980s, and in the EU in the 1990s. During this period, one competitive response was to reconfigure airtime operations on the hub-and-spoke model where major airports are used as the central arrival and departure point for the transfer of passengers nationally and internationally by a particular resident airline such as KLM at Schiphol, Singapore airlines in Changi, United Airlines at O'Hare or British Airways at Heathrow. These changes, combined with information-systems innovation, radically changed the competitive process and led to the collapse of several major airlines, especially those that had no 'hub' of their own and therefore did not control their own supply of take-off and landing slots.

- Technological innovation (cable, satellite and Internet) has brought about a radical change in the nature of competition between worldwide media businesses, while at the same time the convergence of information technology, publishing and entertainment has caused a fundamental change in their core missions. They turned from 'television companies' or 'publishers' or 'software houses' into broad-span giants (such as Time-Warner) that try to maximise their yield from their intellectual property via whatever medium the public may desire. This produced *simultaneous* changes in the relative power of suppliers, the relative power of customers, the availability of substitutes, the threat of competitive entry, and the pattern of rivalry within the business.

These changes can be quite well *described* by Porter's framework — but it is hard to *predict* the moment at which gradual changes turn into a major discontinuity that alters the structure of an industry.

3.2   APPLYING THE INDUSTRY STRUCTURE MODEL

You should now read the Electrolux case study and the 'Note on the major appliance industry in 1988' which are in the Case Study Book.

As you read the texts, try to answer the following questions for the case period (relying on the information in the documents you have been given; do not spend time on obtaining external source data):

- Who are the major competitors in the European domestic appliance industry?

- By what routes are companies seeking to escape from perfect competition in the domestic appliance market?

Case
Study

- Applying Porter's five forces model, how would you evaluate the attractiveness of the industry prior to the Zanussi acquisition?
- What effect (if any) will Electrolux's acquisition of Zanussi be likely to have on each of the five forces?

 When you have completed these tasks, you should watch the case-study video that accompanies the Electrolux case (Video Cassette 1 VC0864 Band 1).

The purpose of this video is to help you to learn how to prepare case studies – but since we have used industry analysis in the Electrolux case as the basis of the demonstration, you can also see how we approached some of the key issues. You should not accept uncritically the analyses which we put forward. Because we wished to make the case-learning process as realistic as possible, we did not conduct additional research, or spend more time on preparation of the case than we would expect students to do. We have also had to make many assumptions to fill in missing data. Thus we are not seeking to provide a set of 'right answers' – simply to illustrate an approach. Challenge our conclusions!

Usually it is appropriate to do several industry analyses. The first would be for the industry as a whole, while subsequent analyses would focus on sectors of the industry. Analysing the industry as a whole provides a broad understanding of the major forces operating in the organisation's environment. The analysis of sectors within the industry may help management make judgements concerning the relative attractiveness of particular parts of the industry, or of concentrating on different sectors of supply (Bowman and Asch, 1996).

In addition to the points made in the video concerning Electrolux and Zanussi you should have noted how the financial information was used to identify key issues in the case study. Remember, analysis of an organisation's financial statements can provide an important signpost to underlying strategic issues.

You will have the opportunity to build on these skills as the Electrolux case is used as a basis of discussion in Seminar Two.

3.3 THE EVOLUTION OF INDUSTRY STRUCTURE

Although an analysis and understanding of current industry structure is useful, it is far more important to project our thinking forward in order to establish how the industry may change in the future. There are driving forces in every industry that lead to changes in industry structure. If these dynamic forces can be identified, and if they can be projected into the future, then we may be able to answer the question – 'What is likely to happen in the markets in which the organisation chooses to deliver its product and/or service?'

 You should now read the Appendix to Chapter 10 of the Set Book.

This introduces some new perspectives to our understanding of competition. You should have noted in particular the advantage-based model of industry structure developed by the Boston Consulting Group.

BCG's model, by focusing on only two routes to advantage, has created a tool which is especially useful when considering:

- likely industry structure and competitive behaviour
- industry attractiveness
- strategic options for industry participants.

The more sources of advantage there are available, the more attractive an industry will become; and the more competitors that will be able to coexist in it, making attractive returns.

The BCG model can also be used to generate insights into the likely risks and returns available from changes in strategy. Industry leaders may choose to build on the competitive forces which have already made them successful, while inferior contenders normally have to try to avoid head-on competition. However, leaders, as well as weaker organisations, are all constrained to an extent by the sources of advantage which are available in their particular industry.

3.3.1 Using industry structure analysis in corporate strategy

In the introduction to Chapter 3 in the Set Book, Grant indicates that the distinction between corporate strategy and business strategy is relevant in determining why we are undertaking an analysis of the structure of the industry. Like Grant, our course is primarily focused on business strategy – how profits can be made within an industry. In Book 9 we will discuss the type of investment and competitive strategic decisions at the heart of corporate strategy. For now, however, it is useful to note that Porter's framework may well help firms to make decisions about which industries are attractive and which, therefore, might be worth entering or exiting. We say 'might' here because there is, in turn, a market in industry entry and exit opportunities: the actual attractiveness of an industry in outcome will depend on how other, potential new entrants behave, how existing competitors retaliate, and whether it is feasible for competitors or new entrants to exit subsequently:

> It is, at first sight, obvious that rapidly growing markets, such as those for financial services or electronics, are more attractive than declining markets, such as those for steel or tobacco. Yet it is the very obviousness of the proposition that is the problem. If these markets are objectively attractive, then they are attractive to everyone, and that will reduce industry profitability as quickly as entry can occur. To identify an industry as attractive is to say no more than to say that Glaxo is a good share or the Polish Zloty is a weak currency. It does not follow that a firm should enter an attractive market any more than investors should buy Glaxo or sell Zlotys. The issue is how much of that attractiveness, or lack of it, is already discounted.
>
> *(Kay, 1993, p. 177)*

3.4 DOES INDUSTRY STRUCTURE MATTER?

Whatever models are used, it must be recognised that they are limited in their scope, and do *not* set out prescriptive rules. In fact, the reverse may sometimes be true. For example, would your industry analysis reach similar conclusions if you used the BCG matrix instead of Porter's model?

As we stress throughout B820, success can come from decisions which fly in the face of industry orthodoxy (Bharadwaj *et al.*, 1993). Industry models do not seek to explain all (or even most) of the variations in returns between different firms. Because each model can be a re-grouping of only some of the forces enabling an escape from perfect competition, individual organisations must logically always have other resources that they can call on, in order to secure advantage. Industry structure is only a starting point for analysis.

Rumelt (1991) suggests that 'stable industry effects' account for 8 per cent of the variance in return on capital in a sample of firms, while 'stable business unit effects' and 'corporate effects' (which might together be thought of as an indicator of organisational strategy) account for around 47 per cent. This finding has great significance for strategic thinking.

The implication of this is that although industry effects do matter, *most* of the variation in organisational performance can be explained by systematic differences between business. If Rumelt is right, differences between individual firms' strategies account on average for around six times more of the variation in performance than does the long-term 'attractiveness' or otherwise of their industry. As he states, 'Business-units differ from one another within industries a great deal more than industries differ from one another'.

Furthermore, the differences between the rates of return enjoyed by different firms in an industry are *not* simply a product of organisation size or of market share:

> ... only a very small part of the ... business-unit effects can be associated with differences in the relative sizes of business units ... product-specific reputation, team-specific learning, a variety of first-mover advantages, causal ambiguity that limits effective imitation, and other special conditions permit equilibria in which competitors earn dramatically different rates of return.

Naturally, the low *average* importance of industry effects does not tell the whole story: some industries may be outstandingly attractive, and some almost universally dreadful; for these, industry effects will be more important. But Rumelt estimates that 'only one in forty industries' will genuinely have important proportions of their return-on-assets determined by industry effects.

From the standpoint of the strategist, these seem extremely encouraging results. Firms are not trapped in an industry-driven mould. So strategy can make a real difference. But what is not clear from Rumelt's work is how far the stable business-unit effects are actually or potentially under anyone's *control*. The strategy which leads an organisation to high or low returns may be rooted in unique collections of resources and capabilities, which it may be unable to change. Strategic choices can thus sometimes be extremely limited, even if those limitations do not flow especially from industry factors.

You should also think again here of the concepts of strategic intent and strategy as stretch, to which you were introduced in Book 1. They are concepts which reinforce Rumelt's analysis. The quality of strategic thinking in an organisation may be more important than industry structure in determining the overall performance of an organisation.

Thus in understanding 'competition in the industry' it is vital to look at patterns of competitive behaviour and capability, as well as at industry effects. The rest of this book, therefore, focuses on more detailed ways of analysing competition within an industry. We therefore move, in the next section, to looking at clusters of competitors *within* the same industry. This level of industry analysis is often referred to as intra-industry analysis, and we will approach it using the concept of 'strategic groups'.

4 STRATEGIC GROUPS AND STRATEGIC SPACE

Understanding how industries and organisations change over time is much more difficult than understanding the structure of an industry or the strategy of a firm at a specific point in time. Section 3 discussed the evolution of industry structure arising from major changes in industries and markets, such as the globalisation of markets, the development of regional trading blocs, or technological innovation. There is a need for strategy concepts which can help us to understand longer-term industry change and evolution which may be called 'industry dynamics'. Before explaining some of these concepts, we give a mini-case which describes some of the recent history of the European food-processing industry. It should provide enough information for you to understand this dynamic analysis of industries and organisations. The mini-case illustrates further the concept of strategic groups within an industry and how some of the resources and capabilities of firms *within* those groups can wither away over time.

MINI-CASE: CHANGING RESOURCE NEEDS OVER TIME IN THE EUROPEAN FOOD-PROCESSING INDUSTRY

The industry contains all firms involved in the production of processed foods of all types beyond primary ingredients (canned, frozen, prepared, packaged, baked, chilled, etc.). Well-known firms within the industry include Kellogg's, Nestlé, Danone, Mars and Unilever. Within this section, relevant aspects of the recent history of the food industry will be briefly summarised.

Industry development and change

Since the early part of the twentieth century, the European food-processing industry has passed through a number of distinct phases. Each of these phases has been dominated by different sets of capabilities, reflecting particular resources and market positioning, and the relative power these factors have bestowed upon existing firms. These stages of development have been broadly described as follows:

1   Before the 1930s wholesalers who were the agents between the buyers (retailers) and suppliers (manufacturers) were powerful.

2   Between 1930 and 1960 there was a rise in manufacturer power when companies such as Kellogg's and Mars became household names (brands).

3   This was then replaced by retailer power 1960–90 as the huge supermarket chains emerged with massive purchasing power directed against the manufacturers who supplied them, and the wholesalers were squeezed out of the supply chain.

4   Post-1990s there may be a resurgence of manufacturer power to service the emergence of pan-European consumer segments. However, the battle between manufacturers and retailers continues as the retailers too (Aldi, Netto, Carrefour, etc.) move across European borders and into each other's domestic market-places.

At each of these industry stages, different combinations of resource clusters were important and they were owned by different groups of competitors in the industry. These shifts in industry structure meant also that the relative

The food-processing industry has seen in turn the rise of manufacturer power in the owners of strong brand names and of the purchasing power of the major supermarket chains.

balance of power accruing to competitors located in different parts of the supply chain varied at different times in the history of the industry. This process is illustrated in Table 4.1. It shows which resources, behind which capabilities, were relevant at different recent stages of the evolution of the industry and who controlled them, the manufacturer or the retailer. (These concepts of resources and capabilities will be explored further in Book 4.)

Table 4.1   Phases of industry evolution in the European food-processing Industry (Segal-Horn, 1992, p. 105)

Resources Providing	Phases of Development		
Mobility Barriers	(1)	(2)	(3)
	1960–74 The scale economy brander	1974–86 (?) The rise of the national retailer	1990–? The European brander (?)
1 National sales force and distribution	✔	✘	✘
2 Getting shelf space	✔	✘	✔
3 Intensive media support at preferential rates	✔	✘	✔
4 Superior product quality	✔	✘	?
5 Low-cost processing	✔	✘	✔
6 Sophisticated support services	✔	✔	✔
7 Volume discounts on purchasing	✔	✘	✔

Manufacturer power from 1930–60 was dependent on manufacturing economies of scale to support manufacturers' brands. These resources overwhelmed the retail distribution end of the industry which was highly fragmented, consisting of thousands of small outlets ('mom and pop' stores). Manufacturers' brands were created which became household names. These manufacturers' brands were perceived by the customer as custodians of quality and reinforced the strength of the manufacturers. They became the most visible barrier to entry behind which many oligopolies flourished. Between 1960 and 1990 rising retailer buying power overturned the balance of power. As large retail supermarket chains replaced small independent shops at varying speeds in the different European national markets, the relative positions of the food manufacturers and the retailers began to be reversed. Also, a virtual revolution in distribution and logistics gave rise to new concepts such as centralised warehousing controlled by the retailers, not by the manufacturers.

For example, let us just take the first item from Table 4.1, 'national sales force and distribution'. This was a significant source of advantage when the retail end of the industry was highly fragmented, with manufacturers needing large numbers of sales representatives to visit thousands of small local stores. These sales forces were a source of advantage that was costly to set up and had therefore previously acted as a significant barrier to entry for manufacturers. As the local stores withered away and were replaced by supermarkets or hypermarkets, these retail chains used centralised purchasing systems and expected key account managers to deal with their needs. The massive sales forces were redundant.

Competition was now as often based on price as on quality. The rapid development of cheaper retailer 'private-label' brands had removed some of the absolute association of quality only with the manufacturers' brands.

National retail accounts supported by centralised purchasing, warehousing and distribution, either directly controlled by the retailer or contracted-out, dramatically reduced the economies of scale of the manufacturers from distribution, and reduced their national sales forces to irrelevant overheads. The retailer now controlled allocation of shelf space in their stores and thus the availability of products to the consumer, via supermarket shelf space, as opposed to the previous rationing of their brands by manufacturers to small shopkeepers (see item 2 in Table 4.1). Just as retailers began marketing to the consumer, so food companies had to cope with both trade and consumer marketing costs, as well as the rising costs of R&D and technology to support sophisticated new product development. The efficiencies of the retailers undermined the resources and strategies of the manufacturers.

Technological and market changes, together with the consequences of the formation of the European Single Market in 1992, created another new phase for the industry, the post-1990 resurgence of manufacturer power with the emergence of pan-European consumer segments. The historical structure of the European food industry was very fragmented, nation by nation. This was, first, because the patterns of consumer tastes and preferences in food and drink had traditionally varied markedly from country to country. Secondly, the structural and regulatory conditions (including ownership structures and production systems) present in each market were highly varied, creating both tariff and non-tariff barriers to cross-border trade. The cumulative impact of these barriers was to protect potentially weak domestic companies, and inversely, to encourage strong companies to expand domestically rather than attempt cross-border expansion. These trade barriers thus reinforced the relative fragmentation of the EU industry. Their removal after 1992 changed two key elements: cost and demand.

Implications of changes in costs and changes in demand

Opportunities for significant lowering of the cost base for manufacturers included increased efficiencies from production, distribution and marketing, which have already encouraged restructuring and consolidation, with large reductions in the numbers of plants and the numbers of companies (for example, production of Kellogg's breakfast cereal is now consolidated to just two manufacturing plants for Europe). Successive bouts of acquisitions within the food industry have been directed at acquiring companies with specific resources such as strong brand portfolios or distribution networks. A handful of giant food conglomerates appears to be emerging, such as Nestlé (Swiss), Unilever (Anglo-Dutch), Danone (formerly known as BSN, French), Philip Morris (US). Acquisition is being used by companies as a route for making new strategic moves to establish new product/market positioning. Many small and medium-sized companies will be forced to exit as a more polarised industry forms. This polarisation will be accompanied by more cost-based European strategies as powerful low-cost own-label strategic groups emerge.

The second key element driving the changes is that of demand. The greater the convergence of consumer demand across national boundaries, the greater the potential for new forms of competition based on pan-European market segments, pan-European brands rather than national brands, and new product lines. Already this has led to many resource 'swaps' between companies, as acquisitions are accompanied by divestments (for example, selling snack foods such as crisps or peanuts, buying yoghurts to deepen existing coverage of the dairy segment). This both rationalises product portfolios and fills out product lines within selected segments. This conjunction of opportunities to pursue strategies based on efficiencies, together with strategies based on marketing and product innovation, makes for a high level of disturbance of the existing industry structure and provides opportunities for new patterns of competition based on new patterns of resources and capabilities for competing firms.

'Cost-push' is creating pressure for scale economies and major changes in unit costs, in an industry historically distinguished by levels of scale economies largely limited by national market boundaries. 'Demand-pull' is stretching those market boundaries to encompass emergent Europe-wide segments, with a corresponding Europe-wide positioning of firms and brands, and some standardisation of products and marketing (such as the re-branding of the chocolate bar known as 'Snickers' in other countries but formerly known as 'Marathon' in the UK). This represents a radical agenda for firms which have traditionally operated close to their national markets, within a fragmented industry structure. Similar trends may be found elsewhere. In the car industry, for example, General Motors have replaced UK-only brands (such as Cavalier and Nova) with Europe-wide names (such as Vectra).

Sources: McGee and Segal-Horn, 1990, 1992: Segal-Horn, 1992.

Activity 4.1

Think about the mini-case on the European food-processing industry that you have just read. To what extent has it succeeded in making the concept of industry dynamics more real for you? What do you think that the emergent competitive strategies are likely to be, given what you have just read?

Discussion _____

An analysis of the mini-case would suggest that two new competitive groupings (strategic groups) are likely to emerge in the European food industry: the pan-European brand manufacturer and the pan-European own-label manufacturer. The resources supporting these two new competitive positions, and the commercial logic behind them, have been described in the mini-case. What cannot be determined in advance is whether the individual firms within this sector are able to build the relevant capabilities which this analysis has identified as critical for the emerging industry structure. Will Grand Metropolitan (UK) be efficient enough to fight off PepsiCo (USA) in the billion-dollar snack food sector in Europe?

4.1 STRATEGIC GROUPS

The description of some of the recent history of the European food-processing industry will now be used to show how the 'strategic groups' in this industry are changing. The concept will be used to explore dynamic analysis of markets, industries and competition. Such an analysis can also help us to understand the future strategies of firms within a given industry, the implications of industry evolution for current resources and capabilities, and their future resource requirements.

In Section 3 we considered the question of how an industry is defined. However, defining the boundaries of an industry is not the same as defining where and how a firm wants to compete. Structural change in an industry often also means changes in how the industry and its boundaries are defined. This will in turn challenge the relevance of existing strategies and also provide opportunities for attaching strategies that competitor firms have historically pursued.

Part of this challenge to existing strategies caused by changed conditions is whether the investments in resources which the firm has made to support its existing strategy are still appropriate. The value of these investments may be eroded both by external changes (shifts in consumer preferences, legislative or regulatory change, etc.) which may be identified from STEP analysis; or by internal changes within an industry or an organisation (new product or service development; technology change affecting manufacturing, design, distribution channels, etc.) which may be derived from five-forces analysis. Thus, industry dynamics affect the patterns of resource-building and resource accumulation pursued by organisations. A useful way of understanding strategic change is to track how organisations adjust their core capabilities over time to cope with external and internal shifts affecting their industry. (These issues of resource and capability-building will be reviewed later in Section 5 and expanded in Book 4.)

Firms can adopt very different competitive strategies within the same industry. The strategic group concept looks at groupings of firms *within* an industry. The term 'strategic group' has been defined (McGee, 1985; McGee and Thomas, 1986 and 1989) as a cluster of firms within an industry following the same or a similar strategy. A 'strategic group' is therefore a way of making sense of different types of competitors and different competitive strategies within the *same* industry. It is important to clarify the issue of performance. Members of the same strategic group are not equally *capable*. Diversity of capability and, therefore, of performance *within* strategic groups, is to be expected.

In essence, membership of a strategic group rests upon configurations of resources common to group members. These configurations of resources act as 'mobility barriers'. Caves and Porter (1977) see mobility barriers as locking strategic group members into specific resources and thereby making it difficult for them to acquire different ones, or move from an existing group to a different one. Indeed, an existing configuration of resources may (as described in the Woolworth mini-case in Book 1) lock the organisation into an historic position, preventing a necessary adjustment to a new reality. At the same time such resource barriers offer considerable protection from imitation by organisations outside the group.

Table 4.2 provides a range of resources of organisations which are potential sources of mobility barriers. McGee and Thomas (1986) suggest that this is a helpful way of understanding the lack of symmetry in competition within an industry, since different strategic groups will be characterised by different mixtures of resources. This is what Peteraf (1993) calls 'heterogeneity'. McGee (1985) makes the further point that mobility barriers are, in effect, costs of imitation, and without such costs attached to the imitation of strategy by other firms, the concept of a strategic group would be meaningless. For example, in order to benefit from production economies of scale, an organisation must first invest heavily in equipment, technology, training and distribution in order to achieve volume and learning curve efficiencies. So a strategy based on volume and low-cost production is not easily imitated.

Table 4.2 Possible sources of mobility barriers		
Market-related	**Industry supply characteristics**	**Characteristics of firms**
Product line	Economies of scale:	Ownership (e.g. public, private, state-owned)
User technologies	• production	
Market segmentation	• marketing	Organisation structure
Distribution channels	• administration	Control systems
Brand names	Manufacturing process	Management skills
Geographic coverage	R&D capability	Boundaries of firms:
Selling systems	Marketing and distribution systems	• diversification
		• vertical integration
		Firm size
		Relationships with influence groups
		Know-how, skills, expertise, routines

4.2   STRATEGIC SPACE AND INDUSTRY DYNAMICS

In most industries there is a relatively small number of strategic groups, representing differences in types of strategies within each industry. To give an extreme example, in a pure monopoly situation the number of strategic groups in that industry will be one. In more competitive market-places, it is still feasible that any particular strategic group could contain only one firm, although several in any group is more usual. Strategic group analysis offers a 'map' of an industry based on the most significant dimensions of competitive strategy within that industry.

Remember that since these dimensions will vary from industry to industry, the axes on strategic group maps will almost certainly be different for different industries. It is up to the strategist, using industry knowledge, to select those axes that most accurately capture the driving factors in each industry. For example, if we think about Glaxo in the mini-case in Book 1, we may choose R&D expenditure as a percentage of sales and geographic distribution coverage as our two axes in a map of the pharmaceutical industry.

Figure 4.1 provides an example of a strategic group 'map' for the European food-processing industry in the 1980s. Such a map should indicate the positioning of the various strategic groups and reflect the resources on which these positions are based. However, the value of resources may be eroded. The power of some mobility barriers may decay and others arise in their place. This building and decaying of resources, and the mobility barriers which they support, contributes significantly to explaining changes in industry structures over time (industry dynamics). It also provides opportunities for new types of competitive strategies, based on different types and combinations of resources, as new markets or new technologies emerge.

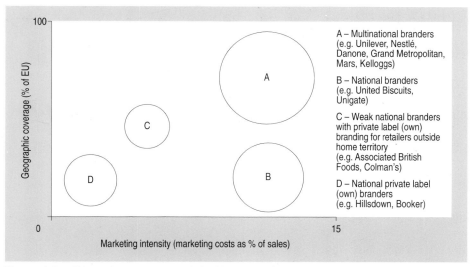

Figure 4.1   Strategic group map of the European food-processing industry in the 1980s

Activity 4.2 _____

Are there strategic groups in not-for-profit sectors? Think of a sector where commercial and not-for-profit organisations are in direct competition with each other (for example, police and private security firms, or public and private medical care). What would a strategic group map for this sector look like? Remember that in constructing a strategic group map, it is up to you to decide what the two axes should be. They will be different for each industry. For example, for health care you may decide to choose (1) range of conditions treated and (2) staff to patient ratio. For pharmaceuticals it may be (1) R&D expenditure and (2) market coverage.

Look again at Table 4.2. Try to list which mobility barriers underpin the strategic groups you have put on your map. For example, the police may have stronger relationships with other influence groups than do ordinary security firms.

4.2.1   Strategic space

Starting from a typical analysis of existing industry structure discussed earlier, McGee and Segal-Horn (1990, 1992) have applied the strategic groups concept to help organisations map their strategies against the moving target of changing industry structures. This approach creates the concept of 'strategic space'. Strategic space captures areas of opportunity within an industry, areas which are not yet available but whose potential under developing conditions becomes feasible. Viable strategic space can change over time. That means that feasible strategies in an industry can also change over time. For example, banks with no bank branches were not a feasible strategy in the mid-1980s. In the 1990s they are not only feasible, they exist.

Therefore, what Figure 4.1 is telling us is which 'space' in the food-processing industry map is occupied and which is empty. Each space represents a possible strategy with a possible alternative cluster of resources. The task of the strategist is to determine which, if any, of the empty spaces can be occupied and provide the basis for a strategy, given the changes in industry conditions. Figure 4.2 helps us to carry out this analysis of the strategic space by turning the map of Figure 4.1 into a grid. This grid gives an overview of existing strategic groups (A, B, C, D) and possible new strategic groups in the empty spaces (V, W, X, Y, Z). Each of these represents potential strategies within this industry. Not all these potential strategies will be viable.

Activity 4.3 _____

Consider the information you have read in the mini-case on the European food-processing industry. Look again at Tables 4.1 and 4.2. Now turn your attention once again to Figure 4.1 and try to answer the following questions:

Is group C still in a viable position?

Do firms in strategic group C have either scale efficiencies or strong brands?

Would you expect B to disappear? Why? Why not?

Will group A become stronger or weaker? Why?

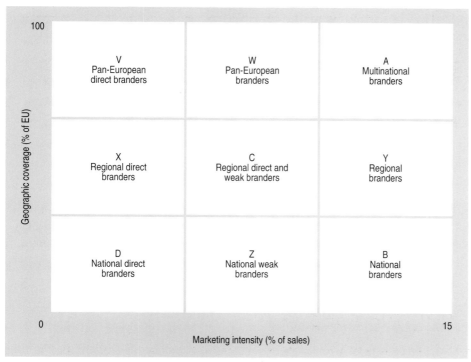

Figure 4.2   Strategic space analysis

Discussion

This activity should give you a heightened sense of industry dynamics and the resources and capabilities of firms, and the relationship between the two. Consider Figure 4.1 once again. One of the companies named in group C is Colman's. In 1995, Colman's was sold to Unilever, a group A company. This should reinforce the analysis you have just made in Activity 4.3 by showing you that this is not just a theoretical exercise. Real companies are in positions within strategic groups A, B, C and D and they are struggling to pursue viable strategies under changing industry conditions. As a group C company, Colman's was not big enough to survive alone. It lacked sufficient resources to build its brands internationally. In the longer term, groups C and D are likely to disappear while A and B remain strong. V and W are likely to replace C and D.

We said earlier that the strategist's task is to determine if a strategic space can be occupied. A space may be unoccupied because it does not represent a viable strategy (for example, the technology does not yet exist to provide the product or the service in this way), or because the opportunity which it represents has not yet become apparent to firms within the industry (for example, that a market may exist for cheap no-advice share-dealing services to compete with full-service stockbrokers). Most importantly, it may be unoccupied for institutional, historical, cultural, structural, regulatory, market or technological reasons which, under changed conditions, no longer apply. In the European food-processing industry, long-standing assumptions about differences in consumer preferences are changing. You can find customers for pizza or hamburgers anywhere in Europe. That does not mean that different nationalities have ceased to have distinct national cuisines. It just means that food companies such as Unilever can sell frozen pizza in all European markets and that therefore a pan-European segment for such products exists.

In precisely the same way, the Electrolux–Zanussi case analysis shows the changing industry dynamics of the domestic appliance industry. It also shows that one of the main reasons why Electrolux acquired Zanussi was to restructure its resource base. Zanussi would enable Electrolux to achieve greater capacity utilisation and greater economies of scale in components.

The concept of strategic space is a way of showing new directions in which investments can be channelled, but does not say anything about the intensity of competition in any one of the spaces. However, if mobility barriers are changing, then they are no longer effectively blocking entry or exit to either new or existing spaces. Barriers to imitation may be weakened (because the amount of investment capital or lead time required is reduced), leapfrogged (by new types of distribution channels such as telephone banking, etc.), or simply disappear altogether ('free' long-distance telephone calls via the Internet threatening traditional telephone companies). The relative profitability of different strategic groups in an industry may no longer be protected by the historic investment in resources already made, since they may no longer provide relative competitive advantages.

It is also worth noting that organisations may simply be unable to perceive changes in rivalry or industry conditions. The data they gather on their environments may be inadequate. Or perhaps even when managers perceive changes, they remain unable to interpret those changes correctly. Even when managers *do* interpret data correctly, emotional barriers to exit may inhibit them from changes in strategy.

Clearly the ability of firms to adapt will vary and can be understood as representing differences in the organisational capabilities of individual firms. Therefore how, or whether, firms will adjust their resources over time is an important strategic issue which is the central theme of Book 4.

Reflection: the sustainability of strategies

In the food-processing industry mini-case, we have been illustrating the impact on markets of changing industry boundaries. The discussion has shown the effect of industry dynamics on the long-term viability of the different sets of resources which have been built up by companies to support their strategies. That is what is meant by 'sustainability' in strategy.

Consider what the 'dynamics' have been of your own industry over the last decade. Have things stayed the same? How have any changes that you may identify affected the ability of your organisation to retain its market share in the markets in which it provides goods or services? How sustainable has your position been?

5 INDUSTRY PARTICIPANTS

The previous sections have considered the structure of industries and strategic groups within industries. The next stage in analysing the near environment is to move beyond a consideration of the broad industry or strategic group to an understanding of the strategies being adopted by participants.

Our objective here is to begin to equip you with tools which will allow you to look at a range of organisations in your industry or sector, observing systematic differences in the ways in which they generate added value, and understanding the ways in which broad indicators (such as financial results) can help you understand their different approaches to strategy.

We cannot understand what strategic options are available without understanding the detail of environmental, market, financial and competitor data; such detail constrains choices. However, it is important to know what questions we are trying to answer, or we will collect too much data. This demands an analytical framework. Competitors' strategies can be thought of as a result of the interplay between their intentions, their decisions, and their capabilities. We will use these categories to guide you through the data-selection process.

5.1 PARTICIPANTS: INTENTIONS

Organisations seek to compete in many different ways. These ways partly reflect the vision that managers have of their own organisations, and partly their vision of the market. So we have to try to understand these perceptions.

Part of the process of understanding competitors' intentions can be undertaken simply by paying close attention to the published remarks of leading figures in the organisations (as reported in the press, and readily retrieved via on-line data services). Additional information can be obtained by looking at annual reports (and especially the statements at the start of the report), and by studying official statements of company philosophy (such as mission statements). You have already looked in greater detail at this issue of strategy and language in Book 2.

Often, however, the best guide to understanding competitors' patterns of intention is to understand the ways in which they habitually act. These may both reflect and shape the assumptions through which those running the organisations see the world (Kuhn, 1962).

- Organisations vary enormously in the extent to which they see the pursuit of flexibility and responsiveness to customers as being central to their mission (Williams, 1994). Especially in contexts where market signals are weak or absent, the pursuit of high professional standards or ideologically defined goals can be of overriding importance. Other organisations, even in very similar conditions, may see flexibility as a valuable goal in itself.

- Organisations can vary greatly in the way in which they view the competitive process. Even within an industry, there are typically some organisations which react much more aggressively than others to competitive challenges. Indeed, building a reputation for aggressive reaction, or for being trustworthy and a good partner, for co-operative approaches, can be a major strategic weapon (Rumelt, 1994).

- Organisations can vary considerably in the types of strategic threats which they notice, and the speed with which they respond to a challenge. An example of this is the way in which US car manufacturers were badly placed to respond to the strategy of Japanese motor manufacturers in the 1980s. The Japanese companies deliberately increased the pace of change, shortening design and production cycles, and building in the ability to customise products at low cost to themselves. The US car manufacturers did not perceive the magnitude of this strategic challenge, because it had not been the traditional basis for competitive action in the industry (Womack *et al.*, 1990). This was also true of the slow reaction of Boeing and McDonnell Douglas to Airbus, as discussed in the mini-case in Book 2.

MINI-CASE INTENTIONS

When Sir Robert Mark was appointed Commissioner of the London Metropolitan Police, power shifted from the plain-clothes to the uniformed branch, which severely damaged the 'strategic environment' of London's gang bosses.

For about 150 years, London has seen competition between the police force and various elements of organised crime. But there were, at several stages, major divisions within the police force between the culture of the uniformed branch (which took a relatively intolerant approach to organised crime) and culture of the detective branch (which was often prepared to adopt a position of co-existence with gang leaders, provided they did not stray outside mutually agreed limits). To the leader of a criminal gang in London in the 1970s, the replacement by supporters of Robert Mark (the new Commissioner of the Metropolitan Police) of many of the key figures who adopted a live-and-let-live policy must have come as a terrible shock. There was a change in the culture of the organisation, as the uniformed branch regained the ascendancy in criminal investigations which it had lost almost a hundred years earlier. As a result, 'the number of bank robberies within the jurisdiction of the Met fell from sixty five in 1972 to twenty six in 1973'. A simple change in the intentions of the police with regard to organised crime (albeit coupled with internal organisational changes) severely damaged the strategic environment of London's gang bosses.

(Hobbs, 1988)

It is important to understand differences in culture and intention, when analysing the strategic threats and opportunities posed by organisations in our near environment.

Reflection

Consider the vision you have of your own organisation and its place within its market. Does it react speedily and aggressively to perceived threats or does it share a stable recipe with others in the same industry? You may wish to relate this to deliberate and emergent strategies, strategic recipes and strategic stretch discussed in Book 1.

5.2   PARTICIPANTS: DECISIONS

Intentions can only be discussed in fairly general terms. It is sometimes more fruitful, therefore, to understand strategies by looking at key decisions, and especially at the ways in which organisations position themselves. The structure of the industry sets a background against which these choices are played out. Organisations can and do make very different combinations of choices, against most industry backgrounds. If we can understand the freedom of action organisations have on major competitive dimensions, then we can go some way to predicting their likely competitive behaviour.

But what dimensions are 'major'? One way of answering this question is to separate means and ends. Ultimately, organisations compete and survive by supplying value to customers and adding value in the way they transform the resources they use; it is the means by which they achieve these ends that distinguishes superior performance.

From the customer's point of view, the question is:

> If your product or service is not cheaper than anyone else's, or better than anyone else's, or you don't serve me better or more conveniently than anyone else, why on earth should I prefer you to your competitors?
> *(Porter, 1994)*

How can these ends be achieved?

5.2.1   Deciding to specialise

There are many different routes by which organisations can create added value founded on specialisation – some of which we have already discussed. Some of the most important ways in which organisations use specialisation are:

- *By pursuing strong branding* – Branding is far from cost-free; to maintain a brand involves heavy investment in advertising. But it helps define a competitive space in which image, not price, is the prime distinction between products.

- *By employing a highly specialised or skilled sales force* – This is hard for rivals to replicate. Drug companies have traditionally employed specialised salespeople, with high levels of training, to call on doctors to promote their prescription drugs. This entry barrier explains why major newcomers to drug production in recent years have been companies selling unbranded 'generic' drugs (exact chemical copies of brand-name drugs whose patents have expired); newcomers have tried to fight the established companies by changing the rules of the game.

- *By dominating niche markets* – Rivals could challenge organisations here only at a cost which would not be justified given the small total market size.

- *By cultivating specialist knowledge or skills* – The knowledge may be overt or it may be embodied in organisational routines and practices which are hard for others to duplicate, such as ability to outperform competitors by developing very fast response times (Stalk, 1988).

- *By investing in intellectual property* – Using patents and other legislative protection to protect that investment. The extent to which this succeeds is dependent on legislation in any particular country, however.

- *By pursuing exclusivity in links to the distribution network* – The most obvious case of this is when companies attempt to purchase their distributors so as to shut out rival products. But it can also happen less formally.

The scope for a company to pursue specialisation strategies will only exist if there are groups of customers with very distinct needs, who are willing to pay a premium to have those needs well met. There must, in other words, be distinct market segments. These segments may be large, or may only constitute a fairly small portion of the total market for the industry.

5.2.2   Deciding to seek lowest-cost production

It is important to recognise that sustainable advantage based on leadership in key cost-structure elements does not necessarily imply a low quality of service, or a competitive stance based on low price. The key objective is to deliver those value-added elements which matter most to customers, at a cost which is consistently below that of competitors. Thus, even a very expensive service (such as on-the-spot replacement of travellers' cheques) via extremely expensive technology such as satellite up-links (Bharadwaj *et al.*, 1993) may still be provided at a lower cost than that of competitors. Your lower-cost structure should provide scope for increased margins, which is important in mass-markets, as well as luxury products or services.

Economies of scale have been a major reason why the largest companies (in some industries) are able to produce goods or provide services much more cheaply than their smaller rivals. Fixed costs can be spread over more units of output, so the cost per unit falls.

Accumulation of experience occurs as organisations repeat a process, and become able to do it better and faster. The benefits of experience are most difficult for competitors to duplicate when they relate to the interaction of teams of people undertaking complex tasks; ways of thought and habits of teamwork may be very hard to transplant to another organisation.

If both scale advantages and experience advantages exist, the resulting cost advantage can provide a substantial barrier for other organisations to overcome. However, advantages conferred by experience gains and by size are not automatic.

- Organisations have to work to make use of the learning.
- They will only be able to maximise their gain from experience if the learning can be kept proprietary.
- Experience or scale benefits must exist in an important value-creating function of the organisation. It is relative scale or experience in relation to key functions – not in relation to overall sales volume – which gives an ability to build competitive advantage around a low-cost position.
- Competitors may enter markets or industries and treat short-term losses as the entry costs of investment, if the long-term rewards are perceived by them to be attractive and certain enough.
- Scale must provide cost reductions which more than offset the cost increases which size can also bring. The costs of complexity in organisations can rise sharply with the size of a company.

In addition to scale and experience, cost leadership can come from many other routes. Organisations can base their cost leadership positions on *superior technology*; on *superior operational logistics* (especially if these can optimise key cost elements such as salesperson time); and from a *cost-cutting culture*, where all staff members are dedicated to the elimination of waste.

5.2.3   Deciding to focus

There is a strong conceptual link between the idea of *customer focus*, and the idea of specialisation; both flow from a recognition that there are some customers with distinctive needs, and that the organisation should seek to serve those needs. But it is possible to seek advantage from customer focus (serving a carefully defined range of the potential consumers in an industry) in the context of *either* a strategy based on highly specialised knowledge and skills, *or* one based on the pursuit of cost superiority. For example:

An engine under construction at the Rolls-Royce factory in Derby. Huge R&D costs mean that manufacturers must seek the widest possible market for their products.

- A key competitive advantage of direct insurers (who sell their products overwhelmingly on price) is the ability to choose exactly which customers they wish to accept – thus enabling them to reduce the claim costs of the best insurance risks (such as older drivers who do not drive expensive sports cars). This is a low-cost strategy, underpinned by the tight selection of the customers to be served. It is hard for conventional insurers to select risks in this way, because of their need to serve intermediaries who make their living by catering to a wide variety of risks within a limited geographical area.

- Aero engine companies such as Rolls Royce and General Electric have to seek the widest possible market for their engines, in order to recoup their enormous research and development costs. The number of purchasers of aircraft worldwide is limited, and it would not be feasible to produce for only some customers (for example, to seek to be a purely 'national' engine producer). This is a specialist strategy, but one with a wide focus.

However, the investment in customer-knowledge has to be paid for *by* the customer. The focused relationship must create more value than either producer or consumer could gain by making contracts with a third party. High customer-knowledge is required in order for a focus-based strategy to succeed. Much of the knowledge may be intangible, and hard to transmit to third parties. Much of it may be embodied in organisational routines and practices, virtually impossible for other organisations to duplicate. Thus focus-based strategies often now seem attractive to companies which face challenges to their historic cost-leadership or specialist approaches.

Reflection _____

Having read about the different types of strategic decisions to specialise, to seek lowest-cost production or to focus, consider which of these approaches best describes your own organisation. It may, of course, have characteristics of two or even all three types. Is that likely to constitute a problem? (These issues will be dealt with in much greater detail in Book 5.)

_____

5.2.4   Decisions and industry structures

Competing on the basis of specialisation and focus is like playing chess or Go; innumerable moves can be made, and weakness in one area can be counter-balanced by strength in another. Specialisation and focus offer a route by which many organisations can co-exist. In many industries, and for most smaller competitors, they are a key to creating competitive advantage.

Cost-based competition is an immensely powerful tool; but there is normally only room for one or two cost leaders. That cost leader does not have to compete on price; it may choose to invest the higher margins that it receives in higher levels of service, the creation of more flexible manufacturing facilities, faster response times, more advertising, etc. Once it has obtained a lead, it has a freedom (which its rivals do not) to choose how to price, position and support its products.

Organisations do not have a totally free hand in making such decisions. Their own history and size, and the nature of the sector in which they operate, shape the choices they can make. There is an interplay between the sources of advantage available, and individual organisations' decisions. In some industries, there are few viable strategies. In others, there may be many. Thus decisions always take place in a context; in understanding competition in a sector, we have to understand that context affects decisions.

As well as being constrained by industry structure, companies face another and even bigger constraint – their own organisation's capabilities.

5.3   PARTICIPANTS: CAPABILITIES

The third element of the analysis of the strategic context of a sector is to consider what strategies the organisations in it are *capable* of carrying out. 'Competing with capabilities' is the focus of Book 4. Here we will only consider in a general way the relative strengths and competences of different participants in an industry. Competitor analysis and benchmarking seem hard things to do, and are likely to involve a disproportionate commitment of scarce internal resources; yet if it does not analyse competitors' capabilities, an organisation's own strategies will be based on guesswork.

It is not always possible to secure advantage against our competitors at every point in our activities. The issue, then, is where to concentrate our resources and energy. One way of determining this might be to identify those activities where:

- our organisation can out-perform its opponents
- significant customer-value is being generated

- judicious reinforcement of our position can still further heighten our relative competitive advantage
- competitors have limited capacity to respond to our moves
- we can gain the maximum increase in our relative strength, for the minimum input of additional resources; and
- our moves will not create adverse reaction elsewhere (for example, by lowering overall industry profitability by starting a price-war).

In the public sector, the need to analyse functions in this way is made acute by the existence of resource limits; only by focusing on essentials and eliminating functions which fail to deliver significant end-user value, can additional resources be freed to pursue core organisational objectives. In the absence of market signals, the use of external organisations to benchmark key functions is often helpful.

The more interlocking types of value-generation an organisation can achieve, and the more closely intermeshed these are with the benefits sought by chosen market segments, the greater will be its ability to create advantage. Because this is so, there will be no single 'best' set of capabilities which organisations should seek to develop. Capabilities depend on the market being served; so the first task, in analysing our rivals' capabilities, is to understand that market.

5.3.1   Understand the differences between the customer segments served by key competitors

Capabilities do not exist in a vacuum; organisations need to satisfy the needs of current or future market segments. Different organisations will have to develop different capabilities, if they serve different segments. This will then help the organisations in the pursuit of some future goals but hamper them in the pursuit of others. This is the basis both of the differences and of the mobility barriers between different strategic groups discussed in Section 4.

The identification of distinct clusters of customers with similar needs, who can be served in economically effective ways, is the basis for market segmentation. We need to understand, for each major market segment:

- What benefits are being sought by the customers who constitute this segment?
- How does the industry as a whole approach the provision of the benefits to this segment?
- How does each competitor measure up against this? Do some do things in a different/superior way?
- What overlap is there between those customers we serve in these segments, and those in other segments we would like to serve? Even if they have different needs as customers, do we have scope to use the organisation we have created to serve the other customers as well?

Once we have understood which organisations are serving which clusters of needs, we are better placed to look at the ways in which they are configured to do so. Indeed, these clusters provide the opportunity for different strategies and hence, different strategic groups, utilising different sets of resources and capabilities. This provides the basis for different strategies in the same industry.

5.3.2 Understand the differences in value-generating processes

To simplify this task, we need to get as much information as possible from easily available data. Published data on competitors' accounts is often the best data source available on competitors (though it has to be treated with caution). Once it is obtained, it has to be put into a format which enables meaningful inter-company comparisons – by using the notes to the accounts to re-format each firm's data into a common analytical framework. And it has to be supplemented by the use of whatever other data sources are available.

We do not necessarily want to understand costs for their own sake; rather, we analyse cost structures because they are often the fastest way to get a feel for how organisations are structured to create customer value (Porter, 1994).

Differences in the value-generating process can be summed up by looking at seven issues, each of which can be illustrated by looking at key accounting ratios for each competitor. The seven issues are:

- How far are the market participants locked-in to high fixed costs?
- How well do they manage their production and operations processes?
- Where are the different organisations putting most of their effort and resources? Are some organisations approaching the generation of value in markedly different ways, and if so, why?
- Where are the organisations in the industry generating and using cash? How great is their freedom to put cash into key areas in which they are seeking to grow? How do the cash resources of different organisations compare with one another?
- How well do the organisations in the industry manage their assets? Do some seem to adopt markedly different strategies in terms of their use of assets, and how does this relate to their other strategic decisions?
- Which organisations in the industry seem (overall) to be successful, and which not? How does this pattern relate to the picture given by the earlier financial analysis, and the market segments being served?
- What is the overall trade-off that the different organisations in the industry make between profit margin, use of assets, and debt? Do some companies adopt markedly different strategies? How do these relate to other strategic choices?

Reflection

Think for a few moments about these seven issues. How would you go about getting the information to enable you to answer some of these questions? You will be asked to address them in more detail at the end of this section.

5.3.3 Look for patterns of competitive behaviour

Analysis of capabilities can be used as an alternative way to develop hypotheses about what is driving competitive behaviour, by working upwards from the analysis of individual firms to arrive at a view of 'strategic groups' – for example, firms with similar approaches to the market, similar distribution and similar production processes and cost structures (Cool and Schendel, 1988). However, it may also identify strategic spaces and the capabilities which would result in new strategic groups emerging. The truly threatening competitor may therefore be one which has a different approach to value generation. There have been many challenges in the recent past from firms engaging in focused and precise competition, aimed at only a part of the value-generation process. For example:

- In the UK in the 1990s, the greatest competition to the sales of investment products by life-assurance companies (which traditionally distribute via variable-cost routes such as brokers or commission-based sales forces) came not from other life companies, but from banks and building societies able to sell products through fixed-cost branch distribution networks.

- National post offices are under increasing threat from courier companies, which attack parts of the value-generating activities of the organisation by focusing tightly on particular high-value customer groups such as express mail and parcel delivery for corporate customers.

The impact of challenges of this kind is often made more severe by the existence of poor or misleading management information systems (especially cost allocation systems). Systems of cost allocation to products almost inevitably become out of date as production techniques change; thus the true cost of producing a service or a component drifts gradually away from the cost recorded in the accounts. Newcomers to the industry (or companies which realise the strategic importance of the task) may develop much more accurate costing systems which allow them to price in ways which market leaders find incomprehensible or unrealistic. It can often take many years (especially in large and complex organisations) to understand what is going on, and adjust prices accordingly.

5.4   APPLYING COMPETITOR-ANALYSIS TECHNIQUES

The best way to test the techniques we have introduced in Sections 5.1 to 5.3 will undoubtedly be for you to apply them to your own industry, or to one of which you have quite a close knowledge.

The Electrolux case study does not provide enough information to allow you to apply all the techniques and perspectives, even with regard to Electrolux itself; and data on other companies is very thin. However, it does provide enough information for some of the perspectives we have introduced in this section to be applied.

The case study video showed some of the techniques that Course Team members employed in analysing the Electrolux case. Our objective was to identify, from the data available in the case, the 'critical points' for competitive success in the domestic appliance market.

 You should now quickly re-read the case material and look at the case study video again, focusing on the comments about Electrolux made by the speakers.

The next few pages set out our analysis of the case.

First, we tried to ascertain the sources of Zanussi's cash-flow problems:

- Examination of the trading accounts for Zanussi, in the period prior to the acquisition, led to the conclusion that Zanussi's operations were more successful than the text of the case study seemed to imply. The operating profit of the consolidated group actually fell after the acquisition, as a percentage of combined turnover: Zanussi achieved 9 per cent in 1983, while the combined group achieved 8 per cent in 1985 and only 6 per cent in the two years after that.

- Zanussi's main problem seemed to lie in asset management issues, and a consequent expansion of debt and debt-service problems. It seemed to manage its inventory control quite aggressively in the period 1980–1983 (inventory days on hand fell from 92 days at the start of the period to 67 days at the end; the figure reduced year-on-year). Other current assets (probably receivables) remained roughly constant in relation to sales. But the company almost doubled its amount of fixed assets (plant and equipment) between 1981 and 1983, while sales rose by only 21 per cent; the plant turnover ratio fell from 2.81 to 1.81 as a result. This expenditure on plant was largely financed by debt (long-term liabilities, which rose by about 60 per cent). Debt service charges rose by around 30 per cent also, and this was enough to very sharply reduce the profits of the company.

Then we moved on to consider the implications of this for strategy. Our objective was to identify the 'critical points' around which Electrolux–Zanussi should mass its forces, in order to maximise its ability to compete.

- The first 'critical point' for Zanussi was likely to be plant utilisation. Anyone who could make better use of Zanussi's underused plant than the company itself could do, ought, in principle, to have been able to substantially improve its cash-generating ability. The case seems to confirm this by saying that 'Zanussi was a vertically integrated company with substantial spare capacity ... that Electrolux could profitably use' and that: 'In total, the internal plan anticipated shifting production of between 600 and 800 thousand production-units from Electrolux and subcontractors' plants to Zanussi, thereby increasing Zanussi's capacity utilization. Detailed financial calculations led to expected cost saving of SEK 400–500 millions through rationalization'.

- Scope for choice of generic marketing strategies seemed limited. The market was mature for most products, and there was 'increasing competition in high price segments'. Thus it seemed likely that future battles would be fought on the basis of costs, rather than on other grounds.

- Because of the low value-added of the final production process, it would be hard for manufacturers to overcome transport-cost barriers when it came to the sale of finished goods. The opportunity to obtain scale advantages in the production of finished goods would be low. Analysis of the cost chain showed that 70 per cent of production costs came from bought-in components. It therefore seemed likely that a major route to securing competitive advantage in the future would come from aggressive management of purchasing costs, including moves (where necessary) to vertical integration. Thus the cost-battle in the industry might be won by those groups able to secure economies of scale in component production and sourcing, and adequate levels of design integration to enable the use of these common parts in a wide variety of locally customised machines. Scale in component production, rather than scale overall, seemed to us to be what was driving the worldwide consolidation of the industry. Zanussi had specific skills in component production.

- The other critical battleground seemed likely to be relations with distributors. There was industry-wide over-capacity, and evidence that distributor power was increasing at the expense of manufacturers in most markets. Data on distribution in the European market was extremely sketchy in the case study; yet it seemed to us that it was impossible to make clear strategic recommendations without it. Although Electrolux might be able to extract higher margins than its European competitors by more aggressive management of costs, these margins might be appropriated by centralised and powerful retail chains, rather than being retained in the company. We judged that the next vital step, in making recommendations, would be to find out more about the factors determining the relative power of retailers and producers.

- Electrolux's senior management perceived the intangible issues of management style – openness, clarity, and honesty – to be important mechanisms for adding value to companies they acquired. Furthermore, they perceived the identification of opportunities, and management of the acquisition process, as being key mechanisms available to them for the creation of value. You will have a chance to consider these issues in depth later in Book 5 on criteria for choosing a strategy and in Book 9 on corporate strategy. But it is worth noting at this stage the very different mission, and self-perceptions, of the senior management teams of Zanussi and Electrolux. It is arguable that Zanussi's critical weaknesses stemmed mainly from its management's style and values, which led to a series of poor decisions; the marked contrast between Zanussi's programme of acquisitions in the 1970s and that of Electrolux can be seen as evidence of this. No analysis of the two companies could be complete if it focused on financial and operational issues at the expense of understanding the differences of values that lay behind them.

When you apply competitor-analysis techniques in the course of your own daily work, you will have far more data than was available in the Electrolux case. Your main problem will thus be one of *limiting* what you study. To help this process, you might choose to revisit the material in Sections 5.1 to 5.3, thinking how far the tools in this book can be appropriately applied. The questions below are a checklist of the most important topics. You will need to focus your attention on understanding the roots of competitive advantage, and on identifying (for your own industry or sector) what will be the key success factors; then to consider how each major participant is placed, in relation to these key success factors.

Some of the questions you may wish to consider in respect of your own organisation are:

Intentions

- What broad goals and intentions do the major market participants seem to have – what is at the core of their strategic vision of themselves? What do they believe to be their key success factors?
- What attitudes do the senior managers have towards risk? What differences are there within the management teams?
- How flexible and open to change are the different organisations?

- Do all the organisations have similar attitudes to the competitive process, or do some seem to view competition in different ways from others? How do they respond to competitive threats? What differences are there between the different competitors?

Decisions

- What routes to competitive advantage are being pursued by the different competitors?

- Do some seem to adopt different 'generic marketing strategies' from others? For example, do some pursue specialisation, focus or cost-leadership strategies? How successfully or wholeheartedly do the different competitors pursue these approaches? Within each of the generic strategies, what specific mechanisms do competitors use in order to generate the hoped-for advantages?

- Which of the sources of value-creation in the industry seem to provide greatest opportunities for some organisations to obtain advantage over their competitors? For example, does advantage seem to flow from exceptional success in purchasing, or managing production processes, or controlling capital inputs, or generating sales, or controlling cost-to-market, etc.? What are the industry 'critical points', and do some organisations have clear superiority in respect of them?

- What market segments exist, and which market segments are being served by which competitors?

Capabilities

- What systematic differences seem to exist between competitors in different elements of the value-generating process?

- Do some organisations have a much higher fixed-cost element in their overall value-creating process, and does this flow through into different approaches to strategy? Remember that fixed costs can derive from a number of different possible sources: capital intensity, marketing intensity, financial structure (debt v. equity), and so on.

- Which competitors (and which products) seem to be generating cash, and which to be using up cash?

- Do some competitors, although serving similar customers in similar ways, have markedly different cost-structures from others? What explains these differences, and how do they relate to differences in strategic approach?

- How do competitors compare with one another in respect of the three key business areas: day-to-day operations, asset management and financial structure? Which competitors seem most and least similar to one another, in terms of the trade-offs they make between these three factors?

- How do organisations compare in terms of the returns they generate to all capital providers (ROA) and returns to shareholders (ROE)? Are some organisations consistently more successful than others in their ability to engage in the creation and appropriation of added value? How do these differences relate to the other issues you have already considered?

6 INTERACTION IN THE INDUSTRY

In Sections 3 and 4 we examined the industry structures and strategic groups which create the context within which organisations interact. In Section 5 we moved on to consider individual organisations, and how they operate in that context. In Section 6, we will look at some of the factors likely to influence the actual process of interaction between them – and the pressures which may exist to lead them to choose competition or co-operation, or some intermediate stage between these extremes, as the pattern for such interaction. Competition is often regarded as a 'zero-sum' game, where one party can only benefit at the expense of another (competitor). Collaboration, however, is usually seen as a 'non-zero-sum' game, where all parties to the collaboration may gain at least some benefit.

6.1 COMPETITION

The course of competition will depend on the particular combinations of industry structure and competitors in any individual scenario, so it is hard to do more than give some very general guidelines. Some key strategies for competitive interaction are considered below.

Surprise is a key means of securing short-term advantage. For example:

- When engaging in acquisition of a competitor, the ability to move quickly and unexpectedly can be crucial to achieving a successful result.

- When launching a series of new products, companies may deliberately disguise the roles they see for each, so as to divert defensive marketing responses towards a wide range of products, rather than allow competitors a focused response to the true product champions.

- Where resources are in short supply, companies can secure major competitive advantage by acquiring control of them before competitors notice that they are doing so. Property and mining companies, in particular, go to great lengths to disguise their processes of site-acquisition.

Building a capability to spring such surprises – for example, by developing a flexible and responsive organisational structure, or an ability to evaluate opportunities very fast, or simply an ability to keep secrets – is a strategic process. That is because it requires cross-functional co-ordination and integration across operating units to achieve such a capability, from which the whole organisation benefits.

Issues of timing are often sources of potential competitive advantage. Remember how Glaxo significantly shortened the clinical trial period by conducting simultaneous clinical trials in 20 countries and also then building production plants *before* obtaining clinical approval for Zantac. This illustrates why the development of an ability to respond quickly is an increasingly important strategic objective. As companies move towards time-based competition, with shortening development and production cycles, they gain an ability to influence the pace and nature of competition, to decide when and where the competitive battle is to be fought (Stalk, 1988).

Maximum use of resources may seem to be an operational issue. Yet the ability to control and co-ordinate all aspects of a company's operations, so that they are simultaneously engaged in enhancing a competitive position, is one of the most important factors in generating long-term competitive advantage. This principle of the 'economy of forces' was described by Clausewitz in these terms:

> If there is to be action, then the first point is that all parts act, because the most purposeless activity still keeps employed and destroys a portion of the enemy's force.
>
> *(Clausewitz, 1982)*

It can be extremely difficult to structure organisations so as to permit co-ordinated action of this kind – especially if the organisations are themselves large and complex. The ability to ensure that all available resources are brought to bear can therefore be of great importance in building sustainable advantage. For example:

- Competitors allege that one of the most important ways in which Microsoft has built its dominant position in software markets is by the integration of its application programmes with its computer operating system; they allege that this makes it much harder for alternative applications to gain market penetration.

- A major advantage of the Scottish Development Agency (as against other development agencies in the UK) was said by its chief executive to be the ability to bring multiple resources to bear – both formally and informally. He contrasted the relatively compact nature of the decision process in Scotland – in which he could know and influence many of the principal decision makers, including banks and other providers of capital – with the dispersed and multi-layered processes facing his English counterparts.

- Consumer brand-management often aims to maintain quite small and insignificant brands, both in order to deny points at which competitors might be able to enter the market, and to force competitors to deploy multiple responses, thereby draining their strength.

Vigour and skill are difficult issues to quantify, but none the less may have an overwhelming impact on the outcome of competitive interaction. The determination and *élan* with which competitive actions are pursued may be crucial. Some individuals, and the organisations they lead, seem simply to be more determined and competitive than others.

Some of the key elements in the competitive interactions described above could be described as either operational or strategic. Yet, to be effective, operational elements must fit within a coherent strategic framework. In fact, it is the management of this interaction between the operational and the strategic which distinguishes between effective and ineffective competitive strategies.

6.2 CO-OPERATION

Hamel and Prahalad (1994) argue that many future opportunities will require the integration of skills and capabilities residing in a wide range of companies. They hypothesise that competition in the future will take place between coalitions as well as between individual firms. They suggest three main reasons for coalitions:

- No single organisation possesses, or has access to, all the requisite resources (human, technical, financial, etc.) to bring a new product or service to fruition. Partners in coalitions recognise that individually they do not have all the necessary skills to turn a vision into reality.

- Political concerns can be assuaged by coalitions. For example, European electronics companies such as Philips and Thomson needed US partners not only to access technology, but also to prevent themselves being excluded from the negotiations which may result in international industry standards being set, for example, for electronic components, TV signals, systems integration or telecommunications.

- Coalitions may help partners share risks. This was an important consideration for the four national companies that came together to form the Airbus consortium.

Coalitions are not static, they develop and evolve. Partners in the early stages of a product/market evolution frequently become competitors at a later stage. Sony and Philips collaborated in the development of audio CD, and then competed vigorously for market share in the market for CD players (Hamel and Prahalad, 1994, p. 191).

Activity 6.1

Review the discussion of competition and co-operation that you have just read. Which best describes the pattern of interactions in your own industry? Would the interests of the industry as a whole be better served if another type of interaction were more dominant? Would customers be better served by more competition or more co-operation? Does your own organisation have more resources and expertise dedicated to competition or co-operation? What benefits, if any, might follow from developing expertise in the other arena?

6.3 CONCLUSION

This section has presented two different approaches to competitive dynamics.

The first was based primarily on a view of zero-sum competition; its focus was on the strategic need to develop the ability to out-manoeuvre and outrun competitors when it came to head-on conflict. The topics were derived from Book III of Clausewitz *On War*; but the themes are still those which preoccupy writers on both military strategy (Summers, 1984) and business strategy (Ohmae, 1983).

The second view was far less categorical in its assumption of out-and-out competitive rivalry. It emphasised the creation of wealth through patterns of interaction with market participants (who might at times even include direct rivals); although zero-sum conflict could and would happen from time to time, it was by no means inevitable; and winning zero-sum conflicts might not, in the long run, provide a secure foundation for the creation of competitive advantage.

Although these approaches to competitive dynamics appear to be in conflict, the clash is more apparent than real.

- It is a matter of timing. At any one time, firms will be attempting to secure longer-term value-generating relationships with some market participants, while simultaneously pursuing short-term gains against others.

- It is also a matter of industry structure. Some industries offer considerable scope for value generation through co-operative relationships, others offer little.

Finally, it is a matter of the purpose (competition or collaboration) for which we are using the models; all models distort reality, and we should be aware that we are using them as investigative tools, to pose questions rather than to advance solutions.

You should use the models and frameworks with care when you apply them to your own industry. They should not, for example, be considered in isolation from the industry structure analysis, or from the study of the value-generating process of individual organisations. As we have said from the outset, our aim is to help you to develop your capacity for strategic thinking; but only you can decide how and when to apply specific tools to situations you face, using your own knowledge and experience.

7 SUMMARY AND CONCLUSION

This book has used three different stages in seeking to develop your understanding of the external environment in which your organisation operates.

- A review of industry structure (which set the context).
- An overview of ways in which you could analyse the different strategic stances of organisations within an industry.
- A brief introduction to some tools you could use to consider the likely patterns of interaction between those organisations (and especially of the forces likely to drive co-operation, or competition, between them).

The research by Stopford and Baden-Fuller (1990) on corporate rejuvenation, which we referred to in the introduction, showed that organisation structure affects the information managers seek and the internal systems for providing it. Managers were often asking the wrong questions and collecting the wrong information. They found that asking new questions revealed the limitations of the available information. They also noted that challenging past beliefs was crucial to developing an ability to seek innovative ways of managing inherent dilemmas in competitive strategy.

A comprehensive analysis of the competitive environment involves addressing the basic question, 'What changes in demand, competitive behaviour and industry structures are likely to emerge?', and might follow this formula. First, the management team share their understanding of the three aspects above, followed by broadly agreeing on the future development of the competitive environment. Secondly, the techniques and ideas discussed in this book can be used to modify and challenge the shared assumptions of the group. Involving other groups in these approaches will increase the chances that challenges to the accepted wisdom will emerge.

It has been suggested (Bowman and Asch, 1996) that by combining an experience-based approach with structured analytical techniques, a useful synthesis can emerge that incorporates the benefits of managerial experience and challenges taken-for-granted assumptions. Because the process starts and ends with basic questions facing the organisations (What markets are we competing in? What is likely to happen in the markets in which we choose to compete?), and because it incorporates managerial experience (which is challenged by analytical approaches), the outcomes of the appraisal of the external environment are more likely to be incorporated into the strategy-making process.

Competitive strategy is not a field in which there are off-the-shelf answers. That is why we have concentrated, in this book, on giving you a variety of intellectual tools to help examine particular situations. Their major role is to help you challenge industry wisdom, to consider alternative possibilities, and to suggest possible avenues of enquiry. The sophistication and confidence with which you do this is something that will grow with experience – and with the learning you will undertake throughout the remainder of B820. Case studies, as well as theoretical knowledge, will play a key role in enabling this growth.

REFERENCES

Asch, D. and Kaye, G.R. (1996) *Financial Planning: profit improvement through modelling*, London, Kogan Page.

Bharadwaj, S.G., Varadarajan, P.R. and Fahy, J. (1993) 'Sustainable competitive advantage in service industries: a conceptual model and research propositions', *Journal of Marketing*, Vol. 3, No. 4, October 1993, pp. 83–99.

Bowman, C. and Asch, D. (1996) *Managing Strategy*, London, Macmillan.

Caves, R. and Porter, M.E. (1977) 'From entry barriers to mobility barriers', *Quarterly Journal of Economics*, Vol. 91.

Clausewitz, Karl von (1982) *On War*, translated by Col. K. Graham 1908 from the 1832 original. New edition edited by Anatol Rapaport, 1982, London, Penguin.

Cool, K. and Schendel, D. (1988) 'Performance differences among strategic group members', *Strategic Management Journal*, Vol. 9, pp.207–23.

Fahey, L. and Narayanan, V.K. (1986) *Macroenvironmental Analysis for Strategic Management*, St Paul, MN, West Publishing.

Hamel G. and Prahalad, C.K. (1994) *Competing for the Future*, Boston, MA, Harvard Business School Press.

Hobbs, D. (1988) *Doing the Business: entrepreneurship, the working class, and detectives in the East End of London*, Oxford, Oxford University Press.

Kay, J. (1993) *Foundations of Corporate Success*, Oxford, Oxford University Press.

Kotler, P. (1980) *Marketing Management: analysis planning and control*, Englewood Cliffs, NJ, Prentice-Hall.

Kuhn, T.S. (1962) *The Structure of Scientific Revolutions*, Chicago, University of Chicago Press.

McGee, J. (1985) 'Strategic groups: a bridge between industry structure and strategic management?' in Thomas, H. and Gardner, D. (eds), *Strategic Marketing and Management*, Chichester, Wiley.

McGee, J. and Thomas, H. (1986) 'Strategic group analysis and strategic management' in McGee, J. and Thomas, H. (eds), *Strategic Management Research*, Chichester, Wiley.

McGee, J. and Thomas, H. (1989) 'Strategic groups: a further comment', *Strategic Management Journal*, Vol. 10, No. 1, Jan–Feb.

McGee, J. and Segal-Horn, S. (1990) 'Strategic space and industry dynamics: the implications for international marketing strategy', *Journal of Marketing Management*, Vol. 6, No. 3, pp. 175–193.

McGee, J. and Segal-Horn, S. (1992) 'Will there be a European food processing industry?' in Young, S. and Hamill, J. (eds), *Europe and the Multinationals*, London, Edward Elgar.

Ohmae, Kenichi (1983) *The Mind of the Strategist*, London, Penguin.

Peteraf, M. (1993) 'The cornerstones of competitive advantage: a resource-based view', *Strategic Management Journal*, Vol. 14, pp. 179–191.

Porter, M.E. (1980) *Competitive Strategy: techniques for analysing industries and competitors*, New York, The Free Press.

Porter, M.E. (1994) 'Towards a dynamic theory of strategy', in Rumelt, R.P., Schendel, E.E. and Teece, D.J. (eds) *Fundamental Issues in Strategy*, Boston, MA, Harvard Business School Press.

Rumelt, R.J. (1991) 'How much does industry matter?' *Strategic Management Journal*, Vol. 12, No. 3, March 1991, pp. 167–185.

Rumelt, R.J. (1994) 'Fundamental issues in strategy', in Rumelt, R.P., Schendel, D.E. and Teece, D.J. (eds) *Fundamental Issues in Strategy*, Boston, MA, Harvard Business School Press.

Segal-Horn, S. (1992) 'Looking for opportunities: the idea of strategic space', in Faulkner, D. and Johnson, G. (eds), *The Challenge of Strategic Management*, London, Kogan Page.

Stalk, G. (1988) 'Time – the next source of competitive advantage', *Harvard Business Review*, July–August 1988, pp. 41–51.

Stopford, J.M. and Baden-Fuller, C. (1990), 'Corporate rejuvenation', *Journal of Management Studies*, Vol. 27, No. 4, pp. 399–415.

Summers, H.G. (1984) *On Strategy: a critical analysis of the Vietnam war*, New York, NY, Dell Publishing.

Williams, J.R. (1994) 'Strategy and the search for rents: the evolution of diversity among firms', in Rumelt, R.P., Schendel, D.E. and Teece, D.J. (eds) *Fundamental Issues in Strategy*, Boston, MA, Harvard Business School Press.

Wolfe, B.S. and Asch, D. (1992) 'Retailers squeeze electrical appliance manufacturers', *Long Range Planning*, Vol. 25, No.7, pp. 102–9.

Womack, J.P., Jones, D.T. and Roos, D. (1990) *The Machine that Changed the World*, New York, Rawson Associates (Macmillan).

ACKNOWLEDGEMENTS

Grateful acknowledgement is made to the following sources for permission to reproduce material in this book:

Figures

Figure 2.1: Fahey, L. and Narayanan, V. K. 1994, 'Global environmental analysis', Figure 2.2, in Segal-Horn, S. 1994, *The Challenge of International Business*, p. 32, Kogan Page Limited.

Figures 4.1 and 4.2: McGee, J. and Segal-Horn, S. 1992, 'Will there be a European food processing industry?', Figures 3.2 and 3.4, in Hamill, J. and Young, S. 1992, *Europe and the Multinationals*, pp. 21–44, Edward Elgar Publishing Limited.

Tables

Table 4.1: Segal-Horn, S. 1992, 'Looking for opportunities: the idea of strategic space', Figure 6.2, in Faulkner, D. and Johnson, G. 1992, *The Challenge of Strategic Management*, p. 105, Kogan Page Limited.

Table 4.2: McGee, J. and Thomas, H. 1986, *Strategic Management Research*, Table 2.5.2, p. 150, Copyright © 1986 by John Wiley & Sons Ltd. Reprinted by permission of John Wiley & Sons Ltd.

Photograph

Page 26: Sir Robert Mark, courtesy of the Metropolitan Police Museum.
Page 30: © Rolls-Royce Plc.

BOOK 4

COMPETING WITH CAPABILITIES

Authors: Susan Segal-Horn and Paul Quintas

CONTENTS

1 INTRODUCTION

Strategy is concerned with the question of how organisations achieve and sustain superior performance. If they are commercial firms, then superior performance over time is based on sources of competitive advantage. If they are not-for-profit organisations, superior performance may be judged in a great variety of ways. A school may be judged by examination pass rates; a hospital may assess numbers of patients treated and unit cost of treatment; the police service may use crime detection rates; charities may look at funds raised and projects successfully supported by those funds; and so on. Whatever the mission and objectives of your organisation, strategic management provides analytical frameworks which enable it to focus its resources on achieving superior performance.

In Book 3, our discussion focused on understanding the external environment. It showed how organisations must monitor, interpret and make sense of the macro-economic environment, the industry environment and the competitive environment in order to grow or, sometimes, simply in order to survive. In this book, we shift the emphasis from the external to the internal context of strategy: the resources that the organisation possesses, or may need to possess, as the basis of robust strategy. It thus requires a shift in the unit of strategic analysis, from the industry (or public or voluntary sectors) to the organisation. 'Competing with Capabilities' suggests that opportunities emerge from an organisation's unique capabilities. This uniqueness arises not from the resources put into them, which are likely to be broadly similar to those of comparable organisations, but from the way they are used. Therefore strategic analysis must be able to look in detail at each organisation and identify:

- what its capabilities are
- how relevant they are to the objectives of the organisation
- what new capabilities may be needed over time
- how to build them internally or acquire them from elsewhere.

Broadly speaking, then, capabilities are the means by which organisations implement their strategies.

Organisations may have the same resources but different capabilities. Any asset which exists in an organisation constitutes a resource: buildings, systems, people, equipment, technology, finance, etc. Daft (1983) has suggested that resources are all assets, capabilities, organisational processes, controlled information or knowledge which enable that organisation to develop and implement strategies that improve its efficiency and effectiveness. This confuses the important difference between resources and capabilities. Capabilities are the outcome of using groups of resources in particular ways (Amit and Schoemaker, 1993; Grant, 1991). Grant argues:

> There is a key distinction between resources and capabilities. Resources are inputs into the production process – they are the basic units of analysis. ... But, on their own, few resources are productive. Productive activity requires the co-operation and co-ordination of teams of resources. A capability is the capacity for a team of resources to perform some task or activity. While resources are the source of a firm's

To study this book you need:
  Set Book
  Video Cassette 1

capabilities, capabilities are the main source of its competitive advantage.

(pp. 118–9)

Such 'teams' of resources are certainly not just human teams. They are any combination of the mixture of buildings, systems, people, equipment, finance or technology listed above. In Book 3 you were given quite detailed insight into how the management of financial resources by efficient managers can result in combining total resources in a different way. The Electrolux–Zanussi case analysis looked at levels of debt, asset management (especially the rise in fixed assets and its impact on capacity-utilisation) and analysis of the cost chain and its impact on margins. It then showed the relationships between all these financial management issues and the overall potential resource cluster of Electrolux and the impact on Electrolux's strategic options. Different financial and managerial resources are an essential part of this range of possible resource *clusters*, the combining of which makes different organisations different.

These issues are central to both business and not-for-profit organisations. The *resource-based* approach to strategy provides a perspective on the design and implementation of strategies over time which focuses attention on management actions which are relevant across all sectors.

1.1   LEARNING OBJECTIVES OF THIS BOOK

This book is about strategy at the level of the organisation. This section lays out the definitions and ideas behind the main concepts in this book. Section 2 considers the apparently simple question – why are organisations in the same sector different from each other? Section 3 is in two parts: a set of discussion sub-sections which define further some of the concepts in the resource-based perspective; and a mini-case on an international company to illustrate capability building as a long-term process. Finally, in Section 4, we look at what the resource perspective implies for the size, scope and functions of organisations. Where should the boundaries be drawn?

After studying this book you should be able to:

- demonstrate that strategy should include creating and maintaining resources and the structures in which to use them
- describe the resource-based view of the organisation as an approach to strategy, complementing the industry structure and environmental analysis approach to competitive strategy
- state the difference between a resource and a capability
- describe how organisations in the same sector may be able to develop and sustain different types of advantage from different clusters of capabilities
- identify critical resources and any distinctive capabilities for organisations, including your own
- understand the critical role of innovation in building capabilities
- describe the dynamic relationship between change in an industry or sector and corresponding change in organisational resources and capabilities
- demonstrate that capability building is a long-term process.

1.2 WHAT IS THE RESOURCE-BASED APPROACH TO STRATEGY?

The resource-based view of the firm has emerged as an approach which explores an important set of ideas (see Prahalad and Hamel, 1990; Barney, 1991; Peteraf, 1993). At its heart is the idea that all organisations possess unique bundles of assets, and that such 'ownership' of these bundles of assets, together with the use the firm is able to make of them, determines the difference in performance between one organisation and another, in the same sector. This also means that it is an approach to strategy which emphasises the role of managers in determining how well or poorly they use the assets which their organisations possess.

It must be stressed that in this book we are progressing from strategic thinking at the level of industries and industry or sector analysis, towards strategic thinking at the level of the organisation. The resource-based perspective on which we focus is not about reviewing the attractiveness of entire industries and their profit and growth potential for new entrants, it is about what individual organisations can do to understand themselves better. It gives attention to skills and 'know-how' that organisations may take for granted. It sees capabilities as things that must be developed and built over time. Even if 'bought' as part of an acquisition, getting the old and new resources to work together to produce an enhanced capability (often described as a 'synergy' at the time of a merger) is itself dependent on the organisational capability to integrate two sets of resources post-acquisition. This point was illustrated by the Electrolux–Zanussi case analysed in Book 3, where Electrolux's post-acquisition management expertise is clearly an important capability which was critical in achieving the effective integration of the resources of the two companies.

From this perspective then, strategy is about 'choosing among and committing to long-term paths or trajectories of competence development' (Teece *et al.*, 1990 p. 38). These authors call this a 'dynamic capabilities' approach, to emphasise that the building of distinctive capabilities is a process, and one which must be carried out over long periods of time.

Capabilities must not be treated as fixed, but as evolving in response to the evolving strategic intent of the organisation.

1.2.1 The debate within strategy

In the learning objectives for this book, the resource-based view as an approach to strategy has been described as complementing that of the industry structure approach presented in Book 3. However, it is important to say that there is a debate going on about this view which is, as yet, unresolved. This debate concerns the question as to whether the resource-based view of strategy is a complement to, or a substitute for, the market positioning view of Michael Porter and others.

If the complementary view is accepted, it implies that some industries are intrinsically more attractive than others and that the resource-based view explains why firms differ *within* an industry. On the other hand, it may be more accurate to say that in dynamic industries and sectors, capabilities are the key source of superior performance and profit, because the competition is so dynamic. This view could mean that either the market positioning view is generally wrong, or that it is applicable only to a particular (more stable?) group of industries and that in other industries the resource-based view is more relevant.

Some of the evidence behind this discussion has already been presented in Book 3 which discusses the relative impact of industry structure and organisations' strategies on performance. The work of Rumelt (1991) and Stopford and Baden-Fuller (1990) may be cited in support of the latter view, that the resource-based view is a powerful alternative in explaining sources of advantage over time. It must be stressed that this is a live debate and that Michael Porter continues to put his case strongly.

1.2.2 Combining resources and capabilities

An important aspect of the resource-based approach to strategy is that in order for a capability to be 'distinctive', it must be hard to imitate. We will explore some of the ways in which this can be achieved later in this book. The point to note now is that in order for a capability to be difficult to imitate, it will usually involve drawing on combinations of resources from any and every part of the organisation. It thus extends strategic thinking into human resource management, financial management, organisational development, R&D and technology development and implementation, and so on. In fact, it is more often the way in which organisations combine their resources in bundles that creates uniqueness, which is what we mean by distinctive capabilities. Many of these combinations are a blend of 'hard' tangible elements (such as buildings, equipment, training manuals) and 'soft' intangible elements (such as how well teams work together, the internal culture or the external image of the organisation) which simply cannot be recreated by another organisation.

Let us take as an example the Italian leisure wear retailer Benetton.

MINI-CASE: BENETTON'S CHAIN OF CAPABILITIES

Benetton designs, manufactures, distributes and retails its ranges of brightly-coloured casual clothes around the world. The Benetton business empire began in 1965 in Ponzano, Italy. It was based on the business ideas of Luciano Benetton, who saw the development potential of the beautiful bright colours and designs of knitwear created by his sister Giuliana. Soon the remaining two Benetton brothers were brought into the business, to be the directors of finance and production. From the beginning the business made use of particular resource advantages that were available to them in their local area. There was a great history of local weaving for the textile industry which had existed for hundreds of years. Textiles were, however, organised on a household ('cottage industry') basis. Labour was therefore not only plentiful and cheap, but highly skilled. They could also be employed on a contracted-out, part-time basis. This set a precedent for Benetton, who utilised this flexible part-time workforce as it grew from a small local firm, to a worldwide multinational company with about 7,000 retail outlets.

Benetton used a similar principle in constructing the retail end of its business. As it expanded the number and geographic coverage of its shops, it did so by means of franchises rather than by owning and running the shops. This allowed Benetton to expand very fast, without the need to provide its own capital to fund expansion. Capital was provided by the selected franchisees. Benetton did insist on very tight management contracts however, which committed the franchisee to selling only Benetton products; to tight guidelines on design, colours and layouts of the stores, and so on. Thus Benetton was able to control, without having to own, sales and distribution. This illustrates a principle to which we will return later in this book, that resources do not have to be owned by an organisation in order for that organisation to use and benefit from those resources.

Two other elements of the way Benetton constructed its growing operations are worthy of special mention: first, its just-in-time dyeing/warehousing and distribution logistics chain, and second, its branding/market positioning and advertising. Benetton's retail stores are usually rather small and have little or no backroom storage space. Most stock is on the shelves for customers to see. By linking retail point-of-sale systems directly to the Italian warehousing system, they are able, for re-ordering, to supply stores direct with the lines and colours that prove most popular each season. To achieve this, Benetton uses a system of dyeing grey garments that are being held in store in central warehousing in Ponzano into the requested popular colour combinations, *after* repeat orders are received from the shops. As a result of this dye-to-order process, Benetton is able to achieve yet another resource benefit: it does not tie up capital or risk losing money on storing unpopular stock items in any fashion season. This also enables it to insist on a 'no returns' ordering policy from the franchisees for the stock delivered to the retail stores, since the retailers can re-order what they see is already selling. This, too, minimises Benetton's risk of having unsold stock returned. By far the more usual arrangement between manufacturers and retailers is 'sale or return'.

Benetton was one of the earliest retailers to realise the benefit of using electronic-point-of-sale (EPOS) systems. Benetton used EPOS both to eliminate the cost of holding inventory and replacing it by real sales information, as well as being able to use the information on sales for decisions about current production. Thus, stock was replaced by data. It helped the company to develop switching costs that tied in suppliers and franchisees and shut out competitors.

All branding, market positioning and advertising activities are determined centrally and controlled by the company. Its adverts and Grand Prix racing sponsorship have proved highly controversial over the years, sometimes resulting in court cases (as has happened in Germany and the USA). Advertising campaigns have included the 'United Colors of Benetton' and the social issues campaign featuring advertisements showing a monk and a nun kissing and a young man in the final stages of dying of Aids. Nevertheless, despite, or perhaps as a result of, such controversy, Benetton has been remarkably successful in its worldwide business expansion. Its brand and its products appeal to a worldwide segment of young fashion-conscious people as trend-setting leisure wear. It has been said that if you are over thirty and feel comfortable in a Benetton store, or are *not* outraged by its adverts, then Benetton is losing the focus of its marketing and market positioning.

The business idea behind Benetton's clothing empire is visible to anybody who walks into one of its shops or wears one of its cotton T-shirts or woollen sweaters. However, despite its apparent simplicity and visibility to potential competitors as well as potential customers, the business is constructed around a set of capabilities which are very hard to copy because they arise from the way Benetton has developed over time, and from the way it has invested in and integrated specific resources such as its dyeing-to-order and its ultra-rapid order delivery systems. These distinctive capabilities may even derive from what the company management itself calls the 'Benetton mentality' – a particular mindset about its business, its products, its customers and its management style, embodied in the extended network of personal relationships between the Benetton family, their senior management team and their agents. Benetton may be thought of as the brain controlling the central nervous system of a body which manages an extensive system or network of external companies. Figure 1.1 illustrates Benetton's operating network and the structure of linkages in its business chain.

Benetton has created, gradually, a unique business chain – the linking together of a set of activities which is often called by the term 'value chain' (Porter, 1985 – especially Chapter 2). It is not any one resource, or any one link in Benetton's business chain which is so difficult to imitate (despite the emergence of many imitators) but rather the way it all fits together. These unique, hard-to-imitate bundles of resources which combine to create distinctive capabilities in an organisation, are at the heart of the resource-based perspective.

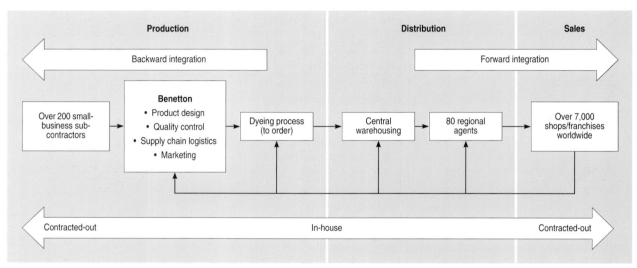

Figure 1.1   Benetton's business chain

Activity 1.1

Having now read some definitions of resources and capabilities together with a mini-case illustrating their meaning in a particular company, you should make a first attempt at listing (a) the resources and (b) the capabilities of your own organisation as you now view them.

1.3   THE VALUE CHAIN CONCEPT AND ITS RELATIONSHIP TO CAPABILITIES

You should now read the following extract from the Set Book: pages 118–123 (the sections on 'Identifying capabilities: functions and activities' and 'The architecture of organisational capabilities'). This should help you understand more about the value chain.

People often find the concept of a 'value chain' rather difficult to grasp. Let us discuss it further. At its simplest a value chain is an activity path through an organisation. It tells you what it does and the order in which it does it. It should also tell you something about how it does it. A value chain can be a very helpful tool for understanding the difference between two organisations which appear to be functioning in similar ways, in a similar sector. That is because organisations can construct their value chains in very different ways. A different design of the value chain, by which we mean a different activity path through the organisation, might simply indicate different ways of doing things, or it might generate notable sources of increased efficiency.

Value chain

Technology	Product design	Material sourcing	Knitting/cutting process	Assembly	Dyeing (100% internal)	Finishing	Distribution to shops
• Knitting • Cutting • Dyeing	(External)	Wool thread fabrics					

Sources of advantage

• Computerised knitting machines • Computerised cutting turning out 15,000 garments in 8 hours, less than 15% cloth wastage	• Computer transfer of design to knitting or cutting	• Economies of scale in wool thread • Centralised purchasing activities	• Decentralised production • Control of equipment centrally • Total production costs 20% below Europe and Far East manufacturers	• External to take advantage of Italian law • Economies of scale	• Main distinctive product feature under in-house control • Keeps 15–20% of stock 'grey' until colour trends determined • Flexibility	• External • Labour-intensive work kept out of house	• Robotised warehouse • Controlled to allow product to be placed directly on display • Minimises shop inventory

Figure 1.2   Manufacturing value chain for Benetton

Value chain

Design selection by agents	Presentation to shop owners	Order collection by agents	Shopfitting and layout	Receipt of pre-priced merchandise	Advertising	Shop sales and reassortment	Cash collection by central function

Sources of advantage

• Allows field-based experience to determine which designs go into final production	• Agents able to direct shop owners • Agents often part-owners of stores (motivation to succeed)	• Time-consuming process decentralised	• Central control to ensure consistency of image • Shop owners have limited choice but must obtain centrally	• Computer pre-pricing and barcoding • Consistent selling price • Tracking of sales possible • Efficient point-of-sale for customers	• Centrally controlled 'United Colors of Benetton' • Consistent brand image	• System for reallocation of stock between stores to maximise sales • Progress followed by agents and area managers • New window displays every week	• Area managers (Benetton employees) responsible for collection of money

Figure 1.3   Retail value chain for Benetton

Let us return to the example of Benetton discussed above. Figures 1.2 and 1.3 break down into considerably more detail than given in the written text, two related value chains (manufacturing in Figure 1.2 and retail in Figure 1.3) for what Benetton does and how it does it. They clearly illustrate the way in which Benetton has designed its business processes. They further show how this unique construction of their business generates advantage for the company compared with competitor companies seeking to provide similar products and service to the same sort of customers. As a result of its particular value chain, which only means the particular way it has designed its business, Benetton secures specific advantages such as 20 per cent lower production costs than the industry average, and fast response times to actual customer preferences for types of fashion items in their shops.

Value chains can be used to identify sources of increased efficiency and also to facilitate competitive 'benchmarking' of how competitors create value and how their activities compare with yours. Four principles underlie value chain analysis:

1   the size of the cost represented by the activity

2   understanding what factors are driving the costs behind each activity

3   the differing processes of competitor organisations in relation to each activity ('benchmarking')

4   understanding the linkages in the chain and horizontal strategy opportunities.

It could be argued that the last point is the most powerful since it is the total way in which Benetton puts its business activities together that has created a set of distinctive capabilities. However, it is also the way in which they have designed each specific element in the chain to exert control over critical processes in-house. Figure 3.2 later in this book is another value chain, a simple construction to help identify and make sense of the path of activities illustrating how the Novotel hotel chain runs its international hotel business. It summarises each activity (i.e. each link in the chain) and then allows managers to see clearly the linkages *between* each activity, the links that make that particular hotel chain unique.

You may find that even a very simple overview of an organisation's value chain gives a great deal of insight into its relative strengths and weaknesses. It is also the case that imaginative approaches to reconstructing ('reconfiguring') the value chain can release new ways of clustering resources and therefore new types of capabilities within organisations.

2 WHY DO ORGANISATIONS DIFFER?

We have already explained in the introduction that resources are the source of an organisation's capabilities, whilst capabilities are the main source of its competitive advantage. For this reason, organisations in the same industry are usually heterogeneous (that is, clusters of resources and capabilities are different between organisations) rather than homogeneous (similar between organisations). This does not mean that every organisation within a given sector will be different from every other in that sector. But it does mean that certain organisations within any particular sector will be endowed with resources that enable them to produce more economically and/or better satisfy their customers' needs. This is usually because such resources are in relatively scarce supply and all organisations cannot have equal amounts of them.

For example, some teachers are rated as better than others in teaching skill, experience, subject knowledge, commitment to pupils, etc. Schools differ in their ability to attract and retain such people. Supermarkets may all wish to situate themselves at locations which have good catchment areas of population and good travel connections. But such sites are of limited geographic availability and will be acquired by the larger retail chains who can afford to pay high prices for the land, or who can persuade local government agencies to give them planning and development permission because they are able to promise a given level of investment or jobs in the area.

Therefore, amongst organisations in the same sector, their approach to, and their efficiency at, clustering resources will determine their performance (their level of profitability and their ability to secure and sustain advantage in meeting customer needs). The resource-based approach to strategy assumes such heterogeneity of resources and capabilities between organisations. This has consequences not just in exploiting existing assets specific to individual organisations (organisation-specific or firm-specific assets), but also for the (dynamic) development of new capabilities through learning and capability accumulation. In fact Grant (1991) argues that 'for most firms, the most important capabilities are likely to be those which arise from an integration of individual functional capabilities'. Such strategic capabilities are what Prahalad and Hamel (1990) describe as 'core competences' and what Kay (1993) calls 'distinctive capabilities'.

In general, 'distinctive' capabilities refer to pools of cumulative experience, knowledge and systems that exist within an organisation and that can be used to reduce the cost or time required to create a new resource or extend an existing one.

They include the ability to access, internalise and apply new knowledge. Indeed, this may be regarded as the defining characteristic of a capability-building organisation. This is because resources may diminish in value or relevance over time, yet organisations may be unwilling or unable to develop new ones. Thus, existing sets of resources may become prisons of strategic thinking ('recipes'). Companies can get locked into thinking of their existing resources and capabilities as unique and fail to notice that what was unique has been copied by competitors,

so that everybody can do it and the whole sector standard has moved on.
Consider the Apple computer company, creators of the Macintosh
desktop computer.

MINI-CASE: APPLE COMPUTER INC. AND THE EROSION OF DISTINCTIVENESS

The Apple computer company had a world-beating technology in the 1980s.
It was the graphical user interface (GUI) which Xerox PARC had invented but
which Apple had brought to the market-place with their Lisa and Macintosh
computers. It was the first computer technology using a 'mouse' to control the
screen and manage the interface between the user and the machine. It was
the first 'user-friendly' personal computer, a computer for people who were
nervous using computers. It used pictures, i.e. graphics ('icons'), to represent
documents and applications on the computer screen. The icons replaced
complex formulas and codes for inputting or accessing software, text or data.
This massive technological change created a devoted and loyal group of
grateful customers. It was also the basis for the classic differentiation strategy
which Apple pursued. It was able to charge a premium price for a genuinely
unique offering.

However, competitors gradually caught up with its unique technology, thus
eroding the basis of its competitive strategy. It was extremely difficult for
Apple to see the extent of the erosion of its distinctive capability and adjust its
strategy accordingly in time for it to make a difference. Apple at one point
was involved in a long and expensive lawsuit with Microsoft, its largest and
toughest competitor. Apple accused Microsoft of stealing its technology and
using it as the basis of Microsoft's world-beating Windows software. The case
was about intellectual copyright and Apple lost. Apple has gradually and
continuously lost market share to rivals who have caught up with its
technological advantage and competed away its ability to charge prices well
above the industry average. The company is at the time of writing a target for
takeover.

To be fair to Apple however, despite the loss of GUI uniqueness, its
capabilities in user-friendly software, interfaces, and multimedia, as well as its
ability to collaborate with and internalise technology from the world's leading-
edge companies, still make the company attractive to predators.

This theme of the evolution of industry structure and its impact on industry
dynamics and competitive strategy has been discussed at some length in
Book 3.

2.1   RESOURCES AND CAPABILITIES AS SOURCES OF ADVANTAGE

Now read Chapter 5 of the Set Book. Note in particular the definitions of
the concepts of 'resources' and 'capabilities' that have already been
referred to at the start of this book.

Also think about Grant's arguments about why the resource-based view in strategy, with its focus on the elements *internal* to the organisation, gives an additional perspective to strategic thinking, complementing that provided by looking mainly at the external environment.

Why does he emphasise organisational processes and organisational routines as important parts of capabilities? Try to think of one or two examples that he gives of capabilities that require processes of co-operation within the organisation in order for the capability to be achieved (e.g. Disney's 'imagineering').

Activity 2.1

Identifying resources

Look at Figure 5.3 on p. 113 of the set book.

Think of a court of law in your own country and try to identify some of the tangible, intangible and human resources which combine to allow it to function.

Now repeat the process of identification for your own organisation.

Then repeat the exercise for your own department.

Discussion

An example from the UK judicial system would be the very old-fashioned (anachronistic?) dress code for barristers and judges who still wear artificial wigs in court. These wigs and the dress robes are tangible, yet they also contribute to some intangibles such as the sense of formality in court proceedings and the idea of 'the dignity of the judge's bench'. These things are therefore both formal and informal symbols. They contribute to attitudes, behaviour and role expectations. They combine all three of Grant's categories: human resources (the lawyers); tangibles (layout of the Court room and the dress robes and wigs); intangibles (reinforcement of the dignity and power of the law by symbols and ceremonial).

You should now watch Video Cassette 1 (VC0864) Band 2, 'The Passion **for Distinctiveness', in which Robert Grant explores some of his ideas on resources and capabilities and illustrates them in three organisations.**

2.2 CONCEPTUAL ANALYSIS OF THE SOURCES OF ADVANTAGE

Organisations differ in their ability to secure advantage from resources and capabilities. That is the basic premise of this book and the underlying assumption of the resource-based view of strategy.

Echoing Grant, Amit and Schoemaker (1993) distinguish between resources and capabilities. They see capabilities as being 'developed over time through complex interactions among the firm's resources'. Amit and Schoemaker argue that *uncertainty, complexity and conflict*, both inside and outside the organisation, *constitute the normal conditions under which managers have to manage*. However, this leaves room for 'discretionary managerial decisions on strategy crafting'. In other words, it is precisely such uncertainties that create the opportunity for heterogeneity between organisations to develop, often as a result of better or worse decision-making by managers about the external environment or the internal resource mix. The article suggests that the challenge facing managers is to identify a set of 'strategic assets' directly arising from the organisation's resources and capabilities. These will be developed as the basis for creating and protecting their organisation's sustainable sources of advantage. The basic idea then inherent in the whole resource-based view of the organisation is to gather and nurture a set of complementary and specialised resources and capabilities which have the following characteristics:

> they should be scarce, durable, not easily traded and difficult to imitate, thus enabling the organisation to secure a revenue stream from them over time and generate superior economic returns from superior performance.

This important set of points about what makes certain resources and capabilities valuable is worth emphasising. Resources and capabilities which are common, short-lived and easy to imitate must be less valuable to an organisation than those which are scarce, durable and difficult to imitate. Rare and inimitable resources and capabilities form the basis of sustainable competitive advantage in strategy.

MINI-CASE: GUIDE DOGS FOR THE BLIND – RARE, INIMITABLE AND NON-SUBSTITUTABLE RESOURCES

A specialised but interesting example of a capability which is hard to imitate and rare, and results in above-average economic returns to the organisation, is the British charity which raises funds for buying, training and supplying guide dogs for the blind. There is a larger British charity which serves the wider needs of the blind, called the Royal National Institute for the Blind (RNIB). The relative success of Guide Dogs for the Blind is explained by the fact that they have large funds which they cannot spend because they are legally only permitted to spend them on activities relating to guide dogs. This customer segment is now almost saturated. Yet the public continues to support it heavily, more heavily than the RNIB which exists to provide for *all* needs of the blind. One explanation for the popularity of Guide Dogs for the Blind with donors is the psychological appeal of the dogs themselves to the general public. This 'appeal' is an intangible resource. It certainly meets the criteria of being scarce, durable and difficult to imitate, and hence valuable. It may outweigh the appeal of the blind themselves who are the recipients for both charities.

A rare, inimitable and non-substitutable resource cluster (see p. 17)

2.2.1 Resources and superior performance

The idea of 'distinctive' competences or capabilities has been around for a long time. Hofer and Schendel (1978) defined them as 'unique resource deployments' (p. 151) which support the organisation's ability to sustain its performance in its existing industries and sectors, or to support it making good in a new sector it is considering entering.

Taking this idea further, Peteraf (1993) suggests that although all resources and capabilities have the potential to contribute to superior performance, 'superior resources remain *limited* in supply'. That is why they are rare and valuable (like Apple's GUI or the emotional symbolism of guide dogs) even though their rarity value may not last forever.

Peteraf (1993), Amit and Schoemaker (1993), Barney (1991) and Grant (1991) all agree that what makes superior performance is superior resources and distinctive capabilities. What makes capabilities distinctive is that they must be rare, durable, not easily substituted and not easily traded.

Organisations with superior resources will be able to produce more economically or better satisfy customer needs. Resources may be unevenly distributed because they are in limited supply: remember the earlier examples of experienced teachers or good supermarket sites. Limited numbers of experienced teachers can be expanded, but only slowly, so many schools have to make do with less experienced teachers and are therefore less likely to satisfy customer needs so well for a considerable time. The case of the number of supermarket sites in good population catchment areas is different. It is a more fixed resource pool which, once saturated, cannot be enlarged. Thus, what is critical is that superior resources remain limited in supply, either permanently or for long periods. It is this which makes them *rare*. If resources are rare for only very short periods of time then the differences between firms will also be very short-lived. What conditions help to preserve rarity?

In order for resources to be durable they must be hard to imitate and difficult to substitute. This takes us back to our earlier discussion about Benetton and the advantages arising from the way it has linked together its resources into combinations which are hard for competitors to reproduce. This is what is meant by the concept of *causal ambiguity* (Lippman and Rumelt, 1982), where potential imitators do not know exactly what to imitate. In particular, capabilities which develop and accumulate within an organisation from the interconnectedness of the resources which contribute to them, will be particularly hard to imitate. These are capabilities which have a large tacit dimension and are socially complex. They rely on complex processes of organisational learning, which are themselves contingent upon earlier stages and levels of learning, investment and development. They have followed certain pathways of development to arrive at the complex resource bundle they now possess. (This is sometimes called a 'time-path dependency'.)

That is what is meant when we say that certain companies have a research orientation or culture. One of the strongest criticisms used against the conglomerate Hanson when it made a hostile takeover bid against ICI was the claim that Hanson had no experience or appropriate skills to manage a high-value, research-based and knowledge-driven business. The criticism stuck. Their bid failed. Subsequently, in 1993, ICI followed the logic of its own argument and demerged itself into two separate businesses: ICI, which retained the low-value, volume-driven chemicals and aggregates business; and Zeneca, which focused on the high-value, research-driven pharmaceuticals business. This was the conclusion of the view that these two represented fundamentally different businesses, dependent on fundamentally different resources and capabilities which needed managing in different ways.

It is also important to recognise that a resource can be *not easily traded*. This may take many forms. A resource may be tradable, but be more valuable within the current organisation than elsewhere. A football player who is a star with one team and a particular set of team-mates may never perform as well at another club. Other resources are not tradable because they only have relevance to a specific organisation. Highly productive and experienced coal-miners find their skills to be non-tradable, with little value in any other context.

Another source of limited mobility is what Teece (1982) calls 'co-specialised assets'. These are specialised resources which are not productive separate from the firm, but must be combined to create value. Consider as an example of this a specialist in particle physics who can only conduct further research with equipment that costs millions of dollars to provide, and technical design and build expertise. Only three or four laboratories in the world provide such conditions. Alternatively, think of rich oil and mineral deposits in the deep parts of the oceans or under the polar ice caps. These mineral resources can only be accessed if combined with highly specialised and expensive equipment, often specially designed for that specific project and requiring immense technical knowledge to use properly. Because immobile resources are not easily traded, their value is likely to stay with the current organisation in the long term.

Peteraf (1993) argues that heterogeneity in an industry is a fundamental condition for competitive advantage. Indeed, heterogeneity is a fundamental concept of strategy. However, heterogeneity is a necessary, but not a sufficient, condition for sources of advantage to be sustainable.

These ideas can be applied to both single-business strategy and multi-business corporate strategy to show some of the implications for managers of resource-based strategy. At the single-business level this analysis may help managers distinguish between resources which form the basis of a potential advantage and therefore attract investment and other resources which do not. Clarity about imitability of key resources which the organisation possesses should help decide whether and for how long a resource can be protected. This, in turn, should influence the decision on, for example, how rapidly to license out an innovation. An analysis of the quality of resources an organisation possesses should help managers use available resources more effectively and have a better idea of the purposes for which they will be used. Resources which are time-path dependent or which require organisation-specific or firm-specific co-specialised assets are difficult to create or reproduce, but since they cannot easily be imitated they are worth further investment and nurturing.

The resource-based model also lends itself naturally to important issues in corporate strategy concerning the boundaries of the organisation, as we shall see in Section 4 and Book 9.

The next sub-section considers some of the special issues affecting intangible and human resources.

2.3 THE ROLE OF KNOW-HOW, TACIT KNOWLEDGE AND HUMAN RESOURCES

Although it is said so often that it sounds rather trite, people are indeed often the embodiment of distinctive capabilities. It is useful, therefore, to explore the balance of power between the individual and the organisation. In certain types of organisation this is particularly true. For example, in professional service firms the staff are frequently described as 'assets walking around on two legs' because the knowledge and competence of the professional staff, and the trust the client places in that professional competence, are the whole worth of the firm. Without them and their positive commitment, there is minimum value in the business. So consider what happens if professional staff leave. There is a high risk that their clients will leave with them, since often the client trusts the individual, not the organisation. That is because a specific individual (or team) will work with the client over time and become the repository of knowledge concerning that client organisation. That close level of knowledge and contact is itself a person-based competence available to the professional service firm.

MINI-CASE: SAATCHI & SAATCHI'S HUMAN RESOURCES AND ORGANISATIONAL CAPABILITIES

In 1969, two brothers established a small advertising agency in London. From 1975 onwards, by a series of aggressive and spectacular acquisitions, the company expanded rapidly so that by 1987 it had become the biggest advertising agency in the world. Its success was such that in that period it managed to tilt the centre of gravity of the advertising world from Madison Avenue, New York, USA, to Charlotte Street, London, UK. It set a trend which has continued in the advertising industry, for companies to build worldwide networks of agency offices to be able to provide global advertising services to multinational customers.

Saatchi & Saatchi made a bid for world market leadership in their sector. The strategy was to provide global business services for global corporations and to position the agency as a brand for quality services worldwide. The rationale was to match the global expansion of their multinational clients. They saw an increase in the proportion of advertising turnover being handled by international agencies. They argued that use of a single agency by clients would be seen as commitment to global marketing and more centralised control of campaigns and international market positioning. It also offered greater consistency. The increasing availability of global media (international newspapers and journals, satellite broadcasting) made this approach more feasible than previously.

In some areas they were highly effective in getting the benefit from economies of scale. Some examples of this would include ruthless exploitation of economies of scale in media-buying (i.e. negotiating bulk discounts for television and radio time or pages of space in newspapers, magazines or billboards) and an ability to attract and retain high-quality 'creative' staff. However, they were less effective at putting other key parts of the strategy into operation, especially those aspects of central financial control that were essential to securing the major benefits from expansion, such as lower costs and operational efficiencies; or cross-selling of complementary services, such as public relations advice. In fact, any tight central financial and strategic control virtually disappeared when their financial director Martin Sorrell left to start building his own rival chain of agencies. This became WPP, the owner of the J. Walter Thomson and Ogilvy and Mather agencies.

The Saatchi brothers, Maurice (left) and Charles (right)

Increasingly, cash from the core business was invested in further supposedly 'related' acquisitions such as public relations, corporate identity, market research, direct marketing, sales promotion, management consultancy and legal services firms. These were further and further away from their advertising agency roots. Nevertheless, for a long time the shares remained highly rated and the Saatchis attained almost 'guru' status in preaching the gospel of service conglomerates (i.e. 'one-stop shopping' for a whole range of business and professional services to be provided by the same supplier).

This came to an abrupt halt in 1987 when they made a bid to buy a British bank. The bid was for Midland Bank, later bought by the Hong Kong and Shanghai Banking Corporation (HSBC). Saatchi & Saatchi's bid for Midland Bank was greeted with complete incredulity and the share price collapsed, putting the whole company into a cash crisis. It became increasingly difficult for them to service their interest payments on borrowings which had financed their acquisitions. In 1989 a new French chief executive was brought in. He had a reputation for tough financial management. Costs were gradually brought under control. Meanwhile, Saatchis' client base and revenue had always remained strong since the agency was well-regarded in its core business. A large number of blue chip clients remained extremely loyal to the agency and to the Saatchi brothers in particular. Charles Saatchi was widely regarded in the industry as an advertising genius and was revered by many clients.

The issue of the share price remained unresolved. Some powerful shareholders never forgave the Saatchi brothers for what they regarded as their irresponsible mismanagement of the firm. Matters finally came to a head in 1994, triggered by an American corporate investor who secured enough votes on the Saatchi board to get Maurice Saatchi ousted as chairman.

This public humiliation of Maurice Saatchi, sacked as chairman of the advertising agency he co-founded with his brother 25 years earlier, led to a rapid resignation of both Saatchi brothers accompanied by many other senior staff loyal to the founders. This was accompanied by the equally humiliating loss of a number of high-profile and valuable client accounts, such as Mars and British Airways. The contracts of employment which attempted to tie professional staff to the agency, and prevent them joining their old boss in his new agency, were virtually unenforceable. Many of Maurice Saatchi's closest colleagues rapidly found their way to the new rival agency M. and C. Saatchi (known as 'New Saatchi'). It has traded very successfully since its inception. 'Old' Saatchi has meanwhile changed its name to Cordiant and sought to attract new business to make up for the lost accounts.

Activity 2.2

Consider the pattern of events affecting Saatchi & Saatchi's human resources and organisational capabilities, just described in the mini-case. Try to think of other examples in similar professional service organisations.

Consider your own organisation. Can you identify some examples of 'know-how' embodied in particular individuals or teams? What would be the effect in the organisation if these individuals or teams left? How could the organisation rebuild or replace the 'know-how' they represent?

2.3.1   Tacit knowledge

The same pattern as described in the Saatchi & Saatchi mini-case can be seen happening in financial services. For example, in investment banks or corporate finance houses key teams often leave (or are poached by rivals) *en masse*. This represents a total loss of expertise in that area (for example the analyst team for a particular industry). One of the consequences of this is that acquisitions in professional services, whether it be an advertising agency, an investment bank, a consultancy practice or a software house, are inherently high-risk. That is because what you are acquiring is the knowledge and expertise of the staff, who represent around 80 per cent of the value of the business and who may leave, taking their expertise with them. In addition, most of this is *tacit* knowledge (Polyani, 1966) which is not easily codified and stored permanently with the organisation.

Tacit knowledge is usually defined as that which cannot be written down or specified. It is embedded in the interactive routines, rituals and behaviours of individuals within their organisations. Many now argue that knowledge, particularly tacit knowledge, is strategically the most significant resource of the organisation (Quinn, 1992; Grant, 1991). That is because tacit knowledge in particular demonstrates one of the most valuable characteristics for resource-based sources of competitive advantage – it is almost impossible for rivals to imitate or replicate.

Knowledge is largely an intangible resource and as such is more difficult to imitate than tangible resources such as buildings or machinery. Nonaka (1991) argues that tacit knowledge has a cognitive dimension in that it consists of mental models that individuals follow in given situations. These mental models are internal processes of sense-making and decision-making and may be personal to an individual or shared by members of a team or a department. We use such mental models all the time in our daily life. Think for example of what makes a good doubles team playing tennis. It is the mutual anticipation of play and moves by the two partners. That suggests some of the reasons why resources of this type are extremely hard to imitate and hence particularly valuable. One of the strongest reasons for the high value and low imitability of tacit knowledge is that it illustrates once again the concept of 'causal ambiguity': uncertainty regarding the causes of effectiveness in organisations. Often the organisation itself does not fully know the precise nature of its source of advantage. This, too, makes the resource impossible to imitate and inherently sustainable.

To consider this point further, reflect back on the description of the cumulative sources of advantage of Benetton discussed earlier in Section 1.3. Rumelt (1984) calls these types of resources 'isolating mechanisms', in that they protect sources of advantage by restricting competition.

Some professional service firms (such as the US accounting and consulting firm Arthur Andersen) go to great lengths to develop internal systems and procedures for storing and reproducing and making explicit such implicit knowledge. They attempt to replicate and thereby standardise and routinise as many organisational procedures as possible. Their manuals are updated continually to disseminate best practice firm-wide. Their content covers every aspect of professional work, such as how to approach a potential client, or how to bid for an assignment. Utilisation of these procedural manuals is mandatory throughout the firm.

Although such manuals are an attempt to capture and codify tacit knowledge, what they actually capture is what Nonaka (1991) calls 'explicit knowledge' or objective knowledge. That is knowledge which can be shared so that at the end of the knowledge communication the recipient knows as much as the provider. This is never the case with tacit knowledge, which contains experience, skills (Nelson and Winter, 1982) and know-how.

Whilst Chandler (1962) championed the view of the top-down hand of management controlling systems and procedures, Nonaka (1991) argues for the middle-up view of management, emphasising the critical role of middle managers in knowledge creation and knowledge capture. To quote Nonaka (p. 104):

> Middle managers synthesised the tacit knowledge of both frontline employees and senior executives, made it explicit, and incorporated it into new technologies and products. In this respect, they are the true 'knowledge engineers' of the knowledge-creating company.

Having discussed some resources with very special characteristics, we can move on in the next section to look at the broader context in which resources have to be relevant, effective and appropriate, both for the strategic intent of the organisation and for the changing characteristics of the industry or sector.

3 RESOURCES AND CAPABILITIES

In the nineteenth century and earlier, most factors of production were immobile across frontiers; differentiated, branded products were very rare; and traders dealing in commodity products were the norm. Most resources were therefore tied to a specific geographic location. By the second half of the twentieth century, different factors of production which were mobile and not location-specific had become critical. Table 3.1 shows some of the differences.

Table 3.1 Old and new critical resource endowments	
Old immobile resources	**New mobile resources**
• land	• technology
• labour	• information
• capital	• brands
	• open international financial markets

As Table 3.1 shows, the old immobile assets and resources have been replaced by more permeable mobile ones. Land is obviously location-specific. Organisations derived advantage from manufacturing or producing at a given location because of that location's particular feature, such as access to roads or ports or especially fertile soil or a raw material. Labour also used to be tied to location and provided special local skills or low-cost labour.

Financial markets then were not global, or even very international, and much capital available was local capital ploughed back into local businesses. Financial capital markets are now fluid, transparent and global, so that even the 'old' resources are now no longer immobile. The new key resources are much more transferable across nations and markets and many are intangible rather than tangible. Many of these resources may be successfully located almost anywhere, as long as the organisation is able to secure its access to them.

From the middle of the nineteenth century onwards, the phenomenon of labour migration from rural to urban areas or across different parts of the globe, has been continuing. In addition, modern communication technologies have made many aspects of specialised labour available and accessible without physically moving people to the same location. Hence the dramatic rise in software companies in India, where skilled programmers are available to multinational companies at a fraction of the salary levels in Europe, Japan or North America. Not only is this a plentiful and cheap pool of highly-skilled labour, there is also a further advantage – staff living within a complementary time zone. That means that the Indian workforce working during the day can effectively process data for a European company overnight. In the same way, 'telemedicine' allows doctors based in Austin or Muscat to diagnose patients' illnesses in the remote deserts of West Texas and South Oman, respectively.

Resources can be located anywhere in the world and the new types of critical resources (such as finance or information) are very mobile indeed. An important organisational capability, then, is that the organisation be able to effectively manage its resources, whatever their location.

3.1 THE ECONOMICS OF STRATEGY: MARKETS OR HIERARCHIES

'A study in the economics of internal organisation' is the subtitle Oliver Williamson (1975) gave to his original study *Markets and Hierarchies*, in which he used the transaction cost approach as the basis for deciding the shape, size and optimal boundaries of an organisation. The argument is a simple one. Transaction cost economics suggests that the most efficient way to carry out a transaction is whichever way will minimise the costs of that transaction to the organisation. Such costs may include the setting up and running of a contract, internal costs of management time and resource, costs of operating at less than optimal scale efficiency, and so on. The idea is that the level of the costs of the transaction will determine whether it is most appropriately carried out internally within the organisation itself (within the organisational hierarchy) or in markets (buy the product, component or service in from outside). When making these calculations it is the total cost over the lifetime of the transaction which is the relevant comparison to make with the cost of keeping the transaction in-house.

This may appear rather a laboured academic argument. However, we have become completely accustomed to it as the practice of 'contracting out' facilities, functions or services to the most efficient provider. This is now commonplace within both the public and the commercial sectors in most developed economies. It is being popularised worldwide as part of the process of privatisation of the state sector. Transaction costs were the theoretical underpinning for looking at the provision of services by both local and national government on the basis of the most efficient use of resources and the lowest costs of the transaction. Should local government employ its own street cleaners? Should schools and hospitals provide their own catering? Should national agencies build and operate power generation and transmission facilities? Or should these services be bought in from outside contractors which specialise in them and can therefore pass on both their expertise and their greater potential scale economies to their customers?

Similar arguments have been explored in private companies also. They encompass not only cleaning, catering and security services, but also entire functions such as provision and maintenance of computer systems, routine data processing functions such as payroll, and even strategically important information systems. These decisions have formed the basis of massive growth in new business services companies such as EDS (Electronic Data Systems) whose phenomenal business growth since 1980 is largely due to the explosion in demand for facilities management. On this basis the entire computing and IS (information systems) functions of an organisation (whether public, like tax collection agencies, or commercial, like airlines) is carried out by EDS for the client. As part of this reallocation of resources, EDS and other similar firms usually take the staff from the client company who had previously performed that function internally onto their own payroll. Similarly, BP has its entire accounting function and systems run by Andersen Consulting. Organisations need to be clear about the strategic significance of such decisions on the overall balance of their resources and capabilities, both current and future.

Transaction cost economics is central to a discussion of strategy as competing through capabilities. What it means is that transaction decisions determine the shape, size and resource base of the organisation. It contributes to answering these fundamental questions:

- What is important that we do internally to secure our customers and markets?

- For which parts of what we do is it better to carry out activities outside our boundaries and buy in?

The answers to these kinds of 'make or buy' question have transformed the size and boundaries of schools, hospitals, local government departments and prisons, as well as companies. Table 3.2 summarises the conditions under which either hierarchies (internal markets) or external markets are preferred.

Table 3.2 Hierarchies or markets?	
For hierarchies if:	**For markets if:**
• economies of scale, scope or learning	• commodity products
• fewer opportunistic actions	• where market mechanism needed
• in thin markets (with few choices)	• profit maximisation and motivation important
• in complex uncertain asset-specific situations	• entrepreneurship necessary
• where information is uneven	• bureaucratic difficulties and/or high governance costs
• risk of information leakage	• routine situations
• strategic capabilities	

The whole issue of markets or hierarchies concerns choices organisations make about how and where to do things. It provides us with a way of understanding some of the reasoning behind the different ways that organisations construct their value chains. It is also central to the issue addressed in Section 4 of this book: the boundaries of the organisation. Let us elaborate on one or two of the factors listed in Table 3.2 to see why.

An obvious point on which to begin is that of doing something in-house if there is *risk of information leakage.* (You may remember this as an issue in the SATRA worked case study.) For example, should EDS take over all IT and IS functions for the police, or is criminal information too sensitive to out-source even if the data-capture and data-processing function could be handled more efficiently? Should commercial printing firms be allowed to print the official publications of procedure and debate in the European Parliament?

The condition of '*fewer opportunistic actions*' means that keeping a resource in-house will affect management behaviour regarding that resource. It may encourage a longer-term view on development of its possible uses. It may encourage more imaginative uses, perhaps in collaboration with other resources. This may affect, for example, organisational decisions about investing in training or professional and personal development. That is not to say that external suppliers do not train their staff. It is more that the nature of the training may be designed for their objectives rather than yours.

Consider a different example. Computer reservations systems are the central nervous systems of the modern international travel industry. They are the means by which airlines, hotels, car hire companies, etc. manage reservations and ticketing services to customers and between themselves. They are also an invaluable source of market data about customers for marketing purposes. However, they are extremely expensive to set up and maintain. Only one airline owns its own system: American Airlines has its Sabre network. All other airlines either share jointly owned systems such as Amadeus or Galileo, or buy transactions from competitor airlines' shared systems. This represents a cost to them and a revenue stream to the rival airline. When the Scandinavian airline SAS was forced for reasons of cost to leave full membership of the Amadeus computer reservation system of which it had been a founder member, it did not lose access to the system. It could access the system by paying on a transaction-by-transaction basis. What it lost was the ability to influence the future design and development of the system to suit SAS business needs. It also lost access to the database that Amadeus represented.

Activity 3.1 _____

Transaction costs and capabilities

Following that general discussion of the 'make or buy' decision for organisations, it is important to think about the consequences of that decision for the capabilities of the organisation – present and future.

- What, if any, activities has your organisation contracted out in recent years?
- What, if any, effect has this had, intended or unintended, on the types of work that other departments in the organisation have been able (or unable) to carry out?
- What does this tell you about the way that resources contribute to capabilities?
- If your organisation has had no contracting out, then for the purposes of this Activity, you should try to identify possible functions or areas in your organisation where this might be feasible. Then you should carefully analyse the impact of any such moves on the rest of the organisation and its existing resources and capabilities. Possible areas of contracting that you might consider have been given in the text. Common ones are: catering, cleaning, payroll, security, training, etc.

Discussion _____

This activity should have made you more aware of the practical relationship between resources and capabilities. Every organisation should be able to distinguish between activities which it regards as core activities and those which it regards as peripheral. Much of the time people do not think about the difference between core and peripheral activities until they have to. The reason may be a change in government policy towards funding (e.g. for schools, local government authorities, etc.) or competition from a lower-cost competitor (e.g. telephone-banking companies such as First Direct offering all banking services to customers over a telephone line without the need to buy and maintain buildings, as required for traditional high street bank branches). Whatever the cause, the effect is to make necessary a review of what the organisation does, why and how. This in turn requires an understanding of its current use of resources and whether those resources are essential to a core capability.

For example, is it essential to education and learning in a school that only fully-qualified teachers carry out supervision of children at breaks and mealtimes? Is it perfectly adequate for medical auxiliaries to set simple bone fractures in accident and emergency departments of busy hospitals? The answers to these questions will vary according to what each organisation judges to be core or peripheral to objectives and customer needs. It may also provide a basis for differentiating between one type of service provider and another within the same market.

A further point to note is that designating a resource 'peripheral' is not always the end of the matter. It may not be quite so clear-cut. Not all organisations feel able or willing to contract-out their IS function or their bone-setting. That may be because on analysing the situation they realise that the data gathered and processed within their IS function is highly valuable market data about their customers, which they would do better to gather and process themselves. (This is what Table 3.2 means by a strategic capability*.) Even more critical are management information systems which gather information from across all business functions to provide managers with the information they need to understand their organisation. Equally, a hospital may find that the ability of a medical auxiliary to judge when a fracture is indeed 'simple' or not causes too many problems and results in expensive litigation from patients.*

We will return to these issues in Section 4 when we look in more detail at the boundaries of the organisation.

3.2 THE ECONOMICS OF MULTI-PRODUCT OR MULTI-BUSINESS ORGANISATIONS

Your answers to Activity 3.1 should help you to understand what is meant by 'economies of scope' (Teece, 1980, 1982) and 'synergy'. Economies of scope are economies derived from integration, from using the same resource more intensively. This means that resources acquired for one purpose can be used for another purpose at little or no extra cost. Technically, that is what synergy should mean in practice. Any organisation talking about obtaining synergies from various parts of its operations should be able to point directly to the sources of economies of scope that will deliver those synergies. Teece calls these 'complementary assets'.

Consider the following example. The charge card company American Express is able to offer a free travel arrangement service to its gold and platinum card-holders. It will make all enquiries as to mode, style and time of travel and recommend best options. It will then book all travel arrangements and reservations for the client. In order to provide this free service to the customer it makes use of the international information processing, transaction and distribution systems that it has already built up to carry out its main blue card business. These are already connected into a worldwide network of airline reservation systems, hotel reservation systems, car hire chains, theatre booking services, etc. All American Express has to do to provide the additional dedicated travel service to its most valued group of customers is to provide a small number of dedicated staff who will tap into the existing network. That is an economy of scope.

Similarly, schools may get economies of scope from having specialist teachers in particular subject areas who are able to teach many different levels of courses for many different types of qualification. The resource is the expertise of the teacher. The economy of scope is spreading that expertise across a variety of organisational outputs.

The availability of scope economies may lead organisations to structure themselves in such a way as to secure those benefits if at all possible. Management expertise may be such a scope economy, in that it can be spread across a number of related product areas, markets or sectors.

Many companies which are involved in a number of joint ventures, or strategic alliances covering various parts of their value chain, may be perceived as 'virtual' organisations. Although they are separate organisations, each depends upon the others for performing important parts of its activities. They have so many shared interests and resources, that to regard them as separate entities in anything other than a legal sense would be misleading. Some discussion of shared or distributed resources, networks and 'virtual' organisations is found later in Section 4. Some well-known companies such as Unilever and Royal Dutch Shell have grown in this way historically as part of the development process of arriving at their present structures. It is now becoming more common for such networks to be not just transitional but permanent types of organisational form.

We will return in detail to the topic of strategic alliances in Books 9 and 10.

3.3   GRANT'S FIVE-STAGE MODEL

You should now return to Chapter 5 in the Set Book.

The chapter provides you with an overview of the concepts and strategic issues that have been addressed in this book so far about the resource-based view of the organisation and its relationship to strategic management. As a result of reading this chapter you should appreciate:

- that resources and capabilities internal to the organisation are the main vehicle for achieving superior performance
- that resources and capabilities internal to the organisation should therefore form a basis for strategy formulation as well as for strategy implementation
- that organisations should therefore seek self-knowledge about the strength of their principal resources and capabilities, *relative to competitors*
- that organisations should ensure that their existing resources are fully and effectively used
- that organisations should ensure that they identify and develop future resource needs.

The chapter spends a lot of time classifying different types of resources, which is an essential first step for organisations seeking to understand their own resources. An important point to note is that 'accounting book values usually bear little relationship to the true value of a firm's resources', especially where the most important resources of an organisation are not only intangible, but also invisible. Grant mentions the take-off and landing slots which are essential to an airline being able to function, yet are not owned by the company. A rather different example may be the 'influence' of a chief executive with other influential business or governmental figures. For example, a Lebanese gasoline retailing company continued to supply all areas of Beirut throughout the prolonged 20-year civil war. The company's ability to do this depended entirely on the chief executive's contacts with parties on both sides of the conflict's front lines. This was the key resource contributing to the firm's ongoing success, although the company's accounts placed no formal value on the chief executive's survival.

Having discussed such resource identification and classification issues, Grant moves to their relation to capabilities. As you will remember from the definitions of the distinction between a resource and a capability, resources are only the building blocks for capabilities. Always bear in mind that strategy is concerned with superior performance. Therefore the important strategic issue regarding capabilities is that it is not capabilities *per se* that matter, but capabilities *relative* to other competitor organisations. This is captured in Table 5.3 (p. 120).

Value chain analysis gives a useful starting-point for identifying capabilities and their flow through the organisation, but it still does not adequately reflect the way in which clusters of resources have to work *together* to create capabilities. In this respect Figure 5.7, p. 123, showing a hierarchy of organisational capabilities for a telecommunications equipment manufacturer, should be helpful. It shows that higher-level capabilities require the integration of lower-level capabilities. It also illustrates the point that capabilities can only be integrated by the behaviour and knowledge of people. It is that which makes higher-level capabilities complex and difficult to imitate. For example, new product development is a *process*, not a function. The process relies on *integration* across functions. The same is true of a rugby team practising its line-outs, or a medical team in an operating theatre or accident department of a hospital. Setting up a communications channel or a cross-functional team does not guarantee that they will work effectively. To work effectively the functional knowledge and individual experience that the team contains must be integrated and co-ordinated.

One increasingly common way of helping organisations appraise, develop and improve their capabilities is through 'benchmarking', which encourages comparison with other organisations. Benchmarking against standards or practices of other organisations can encourage rapid improvements. It is a very useful way to encourage individuals, departments and whole organisations to be more realistic about how good they think they are at what they do. Organisations always have a tendency to be inward-looking and self-congratulatory about how well they do what they do. Benchmarking can introduce a more objective perspective, and remind us that it is not capabilities *per se* that matter, but capabilities *relative* to competitors that determine superior performance.

3.3.1 Sustainability and appropriability of returns from resources and capabilities

The factors reviewed in the Set Book affecting sustainability of competitive advantage should be familiar from Section 2.2. The same categories are used: *durability*, *replicability* (difficult to imitate, 'inimitable') and *mobility* (not easily traded, 'immobile' and 'non-substitutable').

However, the discussion moves on to the further question of '*appropriability*' – who benefits from the resource or capability. It is not always the organisation that owns the resource which benefits from it. Indeed it may benefit more from resources it does not own: think back to the example of the airline and its take-off and landing slots. Appropriability, however, is more specific than that. It refers to the returns generated from a resource. Grant uses three categories to explain this: property rights, relative bargaining power and the embeddedness of the resource.

Property rights over equipment are reasonably straightforward. Patents over inventions and formulas or contracts covering intellectual property are notoriously unclear. Think of the multimillion dollar lawsuit between the pop singer George Michael and Sony, which owned his recording contract. George Michael felt his artistic creativity to be constrained by Sony's management of its music business. He lost the case, but by late 1995 was negotiating his departure to Dreamworks, the new entertainment company set up by Steven Spielberg and others. So what did Sony actually own? It certainly owned all his historic recordings but not the effect of motivation on the quality of his future creativity. This reminds us of the advertising executives of Saatchi & Saatchi. Consider also who owns the 'public service ethos' of local government officers.

In a professional service firm, who 'owns' the expertise of the professional or the good relationship with the client? Contracts for these things are virtually unenforceable. Relative strength of bargaining power resides with the individual. Employment contracts at The Open University clearly spell out ownership of the intellectual output of an academic faculty by the organisation. This does not prevent such faculty from publishing other separate output of books and articles based on the same specialised knowledge. To what extent they are using the organisation's facilities, systems and reputation to help them do so ('embeddedness') is open to interpretation. It is not, however, open to legal enforcement. These examples highlight the lack of clarity affecting implementation for all three of Grant's categories: property rights, relative bargaining power and embeddedness of the resource.

Lastly, the chapter moves from thinking about current to future requirements: the dynamic of replenishing, renewing and adding to the organisation's resources and capabilities.

3.3.2 Putting it all together

Figure 3.1 reproduces the framework from p. 138 of the Set Book: the five-stage model.

The model structures the arguments into a five-stage process which any organisation can use to guide it through the process of analysing resources and capabilities. As you can see this is not a linear model, but a circular, iterative one. Here the loop goes back from stage 5 to stage 1

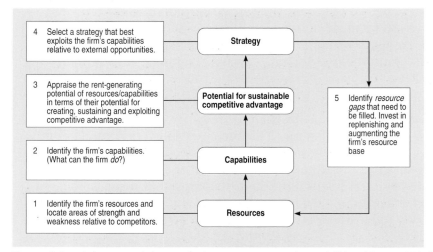

Figure 3.1   A framework for analysing resources and capabilities (Grant, 1995)

every time, in order to emphasise the continuous process of build-up and decay which resources undergo. Resources and capabilities are dynamic, not static. Their relevance and applicability usually have a lifespan governed either by industry structural changes, (as illustrated in the European food-processing industry mini-case in Book 3), or by erosion of distinctiveness (as illustrated by the Apple computer mini-case).

3.3.3   Making it happen

The issue that lies at the heart of the resource-based approach, and which is implicit rather than explicit in Grant's work, is implementation, 'making it happen'. By that is meant the ability to use the resources, structures and routines within the organisation to create capabilities. This ability is itself a capability and perhaps the most critical an organisation possesses: the organisational capability to transform resource potential into dynamic capabilities.

The next sub-section contains a mini-case of a company trying to learn how to do precisely that.

3.4   THE ROLE OF ORGANISATIONAL ROUTINES AND LEARNING IN BUILDING AND TRANSFERRING CAPABILITIES

The mini-case which follows analyses the process of long-term capability-building within a successful multinational hotel chain, Novotel (adapted from Segal-Horn, 1995; Baden-Fuller *et al.*, 1995). It looks at the accumulation of core skills through learning mechanisms within the firm. The analysis provides detailed illustration of the internal mechanisms by which capabilities are identified, developed and then transferred across the company's international operations. It examines the organisational structures, processes and routines that it has created to implement its strategy. It provides insight into the role of capabilities in the development of competitive advantage for an international service firm. Service firms are characterised by particular combinations of resources and capabilities different from those characteristic of manufacturing firms, the most obvious difference being the predominance in service organisations of the point of contact between the front-line staff and the customer. The resource-based approach focuses on the creation and sharing of knowledge-based resources and is particularly helpful for service industries, since most services are heavily dependent on knowledge-based resources in both the design and delivery of the service, and especially on the tacit knowledge underpinning the routines of staff.

The assumption fundamental to resource-based strategy suggests that explanations of the competitive advantage of firms within the same industry context may be provided by exploring the internal processes for capability building, capability management and capability retention of different competitors. It also suggests different processes of asset accumulation and asset sustainability by individual firms. The brief discussion of some of Novotel's capability building and capability management processes is an attempt to get inside the detail of what these concepts mean in practice. It also shows how these processes may provide defensible sources of advantage to organisations that have the capability to use them effectively.

The strategic management task for Novotel is to create processes for meeting customer expectations in all its hotels worldwide. It must therefore achieve consistency whilst still enabling all front-line and managerial staff to deal sensitively and helpfully with customer needs.

MINI-CASE OF A MULTINATIONAL HOTEL CHAIN: THE CREATION AND SHARING OF KNOWLEDGE-BASED ASSETS

The first Novotel hotel was opened by two entrepreneurs near Lille airport in France in 1967. The first Novotel outside France was opened in 1973. By 1995 the chain had grown to 280 hotels in 46 countries around the world. The hotels provide 43,000 rooms and employ 33,000 people. Novotel is just one of the hotel chains belonging to the Accor Group of France, which operates more than 2,000 hotels worldwide offering more than two million rooms at different ratings and service levels. Other chains in the group include Sofitel, Mercure, Ibis, Formule 1. These range from 4-star (Sofitel) to 1-star (Formule 1).

The fundamental characteristic of the Novotel hotel concept is the international standardisation of the offering. What is therefore required is consistency of the offering in every location in which it is available. This means putting in place a system that is robust enough to generate consistent service standards to satisfy customer expectations, irrespective of local conditions or infrastructure. Some of the elements of standardisation are easily realisable. The design, style and layouts of the hotels are reproduced to precise specifications. For example, bedroom size is standard throughout Europe at 24 square metres, although this does differ for Novotel Asia. The Novotel chain is positioned as a 3-star chain worldwide, which means that certain facilities such as quality of bedroom furniture, fixtures and fittings or outside amenities such as swimming pools and amounts of free car parking space are always available at all Novotel units.

Product design	Marketing	Distribution	Service provision	Service monitoring and enhancement
• Hospitality concept • 3-star • Features • Layout • Locations • Image • Homogeneity • NPD	• Corporate travel management • Partnership programmes • Special promotions • Pricing • Geographic network • Advertising themes • Materials	• Global reservation systems • Networks • Travel agencies	• Purchasing efficiencies • Supplier partnership programmes • Staff multi-skilling • Staff exchanges • Multi-culture	• Customer surveys • Quality measures • Compliance measures • Directors' clubs/progress groups

Figure 3.2   The Novotel business chain (Teare and Armistead, 1995)

Figure 3.2 captures some of the key elements in the Novotel business chain. However, the more interesting elements of the Novotel offering for the purposes of this discussion are the management processes which enable the service levels to be delivered at all locations worldwide.

Since hotel design and guest bedrooms are standardised, basic housekeeping and maintenance functions can in turn be standardised. That means that the training of staff in all basic functions may be simplified and training procedures themselves standardised. Indeed, one of the features of Novotel's parent company the Accor Group, is the 'Académie Accor', set up in 1985 as the centre for all staff training within the group. Its 'campus' is located on the site of group corporate headquarters just outside Paris. From there, all training is designed and delivered. This standardised approach to the core service concept places special requirements on the staff as the key medium for delivery of consistent service standards wherever the customer is staying. Standardised procedures and centrally designed training programmes are one of the core mechanisms for securing such consistency.

Taking the notion of consistency one stage further, the Novotel senior management developed a new approach to staffing in the hotel sector which is described as 'multi-skilling'. ('Polyvalence' is the correct French word; however, the word 'multicompetence' is frequently used inside Novotel because of its similarity to English words.) The idea behind multi-skilling is to develop staff as a team able to perform all tasks and work as needed in a flexible manner. Obviously, this has many advantages for hotel management, not least in smoothing the need for certain types of staff at peak periods of the day or evening. Pressures on checking-in or checking-out at reception cluster at early morning and evening. This, and getting rooms cleaned while guests are at breakfast, are common bottlenecks dramatically affecting patterns of staffing. With the Novotel approach to flexible skilling and team working, a new pattern emerged. Flexible working patterns broke down the staff demarcation, normal within the rest of the hotel industry. Reception and front-of-house activities (e.g. showing guests to rooms) were carried out by the same staff who then served in the restaurant at peak mealtimes or performed housekeeping or room-cleaning tasks at other times of the day. The benefits of this to the firm were enormous: a reduction of core staff levels and the availability of a more resourceful workforce. Reduced staff levels also yielded significant cost benefits, since this is a labour-intensive industry. However, maintaining universal quality standards as the chain grew rapidly over a 25-year period became more and more problematic, especially when many new staff were recruited from other hotel groups with different working practices.

A system to monitor standard procedures was introduced in 1987. It regulated the thirteen main points of staff/customer interaction. These were: reservation, arrival/access, parking, check-in, hall, bedroom, bathroom/WC, evening meal, breakfast, shops, bar, outdoor games/swimming-pool and check-out. Each of these key interaction points was divided into a series of compulsory directives for staff, e.g. how to set out a bedroom, lay a place setting in the restaurant or welcome a guest. A booklet containing all 95 of these compulsory directives was issued to all staff and was a mainstay in the induction of new staff. An internal team of inspectors visited each hotel approximately twice each year to monitor standards. They functioned in the same way as 'mystery shoppers' in that they made reservations, arrived, stayed and departed incognito. On completion of their stay they would make themselves known to the General Manager (GM) for review and discussion. Percentage grades were awarded and recommendations made. This system, while helping Novotel to control and consolidate after a period of rapid growth, gradually became over-rigid and procedural in orientation.

At a meeting in 1992 for Novotel managers in an 'open space' format (i.e. where participants may propose topics for discussion, move from group to group according to preference, or indeed, leave) the relationship of hotel GMs and their staff teams was redefined from hierarchical to enabling. A new corporate slogan 'Back to the Future' ('Retour vers le futur') was adopted to reflect the outlawing of the bureaucratic style of standardisation and a return to Novotel's entrepreneurial roots. In addition, mixed level (i.e. beyond just the top team) working parties were established in three key issue areas: communication (marketing and image), management and commercial. Inter-functional groups were set up across hotels and countries. GM groups were established which clustered together special interests across countries, to share ideas, innovations or best practice. These GM interest groups were constructed around common hotel types within the Novotel chain, e.g. all GMs of motorway locations or airport locations or city centre locations.

The 95 directives were abolished as too rigid and replaced by three simplified general measures of performance – clients, management and people. All internal procedures were assessed only in relation to these three elements of the business. One and a half layers of management were eliminated, leaving only one direct reporting layer between GMs and the two co-presidents of Novotel. (Novotel now has just one chairman after the departure of Gilles Pelisson in the autumn of 1994, to help turn around Disneyland Paris.)

The role of the GM was rethought and redefined as capturing the spirit of 'maître de maison', much closer to the social role of a ship's captain. This led to a need for reassessment and redevelopment of all GMs, who were required to go through an assessment activity incorporating role-play in such situations as conflict resolution with subordinates or guests.

Whilst great effort was made to position these assessments and changes as constructive inputs for identifying positive training needs, rather than negative grounds for dismissal, this emphasis on new styles of working for both management and all staff created much anxiety and uncertainty which the top team had to transform into a positive atmosphere of empowerment and opportunity. As an illustration of the imaginative ways in which this extremely delicate problem was tackled, two Benedictine monks were guests at one of

Hotel chain Novotel drew on the centuries-old tradition of hospitality of the Benedictine order of monks when planning new working methods.

Novotel's large management conventions in 1993. The Benedictine fathers were invited to speak to the gathering about the principles of Benedictine hospitality and welcome which had graced their order since its founding 15 centuries before. Benedictine principles, duties and procedures were described and explained. It is also worth noting the continuous active involvement in the redevelopment process of the two original founders of Novotel (now co-presidents of the Accor Group), as well as the visible public involvement of the co-presidents of Novotel.

Activity 3.3

Consider the mini-case on the Novotel international hotel chain that you have just read. List the main items of organisational learning that occurred at Novotel.

In your opinion, what are the key capabilities that Novotel now possesses as a result of the changes and developments described?

Discussion

In summarising the outcomes of the process change described above, both the structure and operations of Novotel's corporate headquarters, as well as operations and routines in every hotel in the chain, were transformed, although in differing degrees and over different timescales. The transformations reflect the new roles and tasks of management (managerial capabilities) shown in Table 3.3.

Table 3.3 New roles and tasks of management		
Top management	**Middle management**	**Front-line management**
Creator of purpose and challenger of status quo	Horizontal information broker and capability integrator	Entrepreneur and performance driver
(Adapted from Bartlett and Ghoshal, 1993, p. 44)		

Potentially sustainable sources of advantage for Novotel arising from the changes include the following:

- *Delayering has led to reduction in numbers of management and staff per hotel. Labour costs in the hotel business are significant; so also is time for staff to be available to deal with customers. The benefit is measurable in added value to staff and customers, and in the management of costs.*

- *Information flows throughout the company have changed. Flattening the hierarchy enables more relevant information to be conveyed faster.*
- *The role of headquarters has changed. It now acts as an information co-ordinator, collator and channel, rather than the instigator of time-consuming demands for central performance statistics. This releases GMs' time for driving performance. For example, the headquarters filters useful information to all hotels which they store for shared reference.*
- *Collaboration across and between levels has increased. GMs organise self-help clusters; training sessions are shared across the group; 'reflective clubs' ('clubs de réflexion') have been created in some hotels as mixed informal groupings of staff who meet to discuss innovations. Significantly, they contain staff from across all service areas and discussion covers the hotel as a whole, not the specific responsibility of any individual staff.*
- *The role of the GM has changed to that of 'coach', optimising the service and amenities available to guests by developing the competences of his or her team.*
- *Ways of working have changed for all staff. The horizons of staff have been broadened, giving greater awareness of the business as a whole as well as more responsibility, encouraging cross-functional links and increased autonomy, which adds value for staff and guests alike.*

3.5 CAPABILITY TO INNOVATE

One of the key capabilities that transform knowledge into competitive advantage is innovative capability. This explains in part why some companies are so good at not only developing but also exploiting new products or services. We will provide a formal definition of an innovation in Book 5 but in this section we will examine the ways in which organisations build the capabilities necessary for innovation.

Early entrepreneurial models of innovation, which focused on the heroic individual, gave way in the mid-twentieth century to a model based on the large corporation. Chandler (1962) documented the efficiency advantages of the divisionalised form of organisation (which will be discussed more fully in Books 7, 9 and 10) in which the R&D laboratory played a major role. Corporate R&D was viewed as the locus of innovative activity, as the requirement for a significant 'critical mass' of research capability began to dominate in sectors such as electronics, pharmaceuticals, chemicals and aerospace.

As the Xerox GUI/Apple example in Book 4 showed, the divisionalised corporation with a separate R&D laboratory presented problems. Roussel *et al.* (1991) suggest that there are three generations in the history of industrial innovation in large corporations. In generation 1 there is a high wall between the R&D department and the factory. The R&D department would invent something, and throw it over the wall to the factory. In generation 2 the high wall is still there, but this time the factory writes down what they want the R&D department to develop for them, and throw the message over the wall to the R&D department. In generation 3 the wall has been demolished, and the R&D and other factory departments sit down together to discuss their capabilities and common needs. The authors note, however, that generation 3 has not yet been reached by many companies.

In contrast to this picture, it is clear that innovation requires organisational structures and processes that support integration across functional areas. The provision of horizontal links between the functional areas of the firm, often involving the transfer of individuals between R&D and production, has been identified as being of key importance in the successful management of innovation.

Figure 3.3 shows how one electronics company plans its strategy for R&D and product innovation. The diagram shows how research is categorised according to strategic value. The left-hand scale shows how sponsorship of the research varies according to the type of R&D. The shading indicates how the company plans its R&D, and identifies those areas it avoids. The company makes a key distinction between *generic* research, which may be applicable across a range of product-markets, and product-specific research and development. Generic research is funded from central funds, which are gathered by a levy across all divisions.

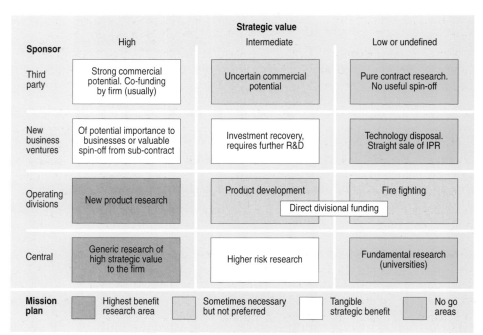

Figure 3.3   R&D strategy in an electronics company

Activity 3.4

Where does the strategy in Figure 3.3 look most vulnerable?

Discussion

The strategy exemplified in Figure 3.3 shows some weakness in the area of R&D with 'uncertain commercial potential'. As we noted earlier, organisations may be vulnerable to technology that comes from outside their current expertise and R&D focus. This was illustrated by many examples, including the pharmaceuticals industry in relation to biotechnology.

One way of thinking strategically about this problem is to distinguish between *core* and *peripheral* technology. The core technology of an organisation is that which forms the basis of current activities, and therefore it is the area in which it must continually maintain a core capability. Peripheral technology is on the edge of current mainstream activity and capability. However, the problem is that technology regarded as being peripheral today may, over time, become the basis of the future core business. Organisations must find ways of tracking new technological developments whilst maintaining capabilities in their core technology areas. This presents challenges in generating the resources and developing the expertise to do this.

Innovation results from inputs of all kinds of knowledge or intellectual capital, including the know-how and expertise accumulated by individuals. Much of this knowledge in individuals is not captured by any formal systems – it is tacit knowledge that is difficult to codify. Other forms of knowledge, such as design briefs, specifications, patents, manuals of procedures and guidelines, are written down or otherwise codified, and therefore easier to transfer between individuals, departments and organisations, or reproduced over time. Tacit knowledge is recognised as valuable, but few organisations have management tools which enable them to evaluate, grow, protect and value informal and tacit knowledge.

Organisations must find ways to orchestrate the knowledge inputs to innovation. They must decide what they need to 'own', and what they can afford to subcontract, buy in, or acquire through alliances or other means. One major requirement for innovation to occur concerns the transfer and assimilation of knowledge.

Pavitt (1989) emphasises that the cost of assimilating knowledge and technologies from outside a firm is very high. The knowledge applied by commercial enterprises tends to be firm-specific and cumulative. Corporate technological competences are built over many years through R&D and 'learning-by-doing' processes, and thus often involve tacit skills which are not easily transferable. This view has recently been confirmed in a detailed international study of the opto-electronics industry (Miyazaki, 1995).

One of the reasons why firms undertake R&D is in order to be able to track external developments and to assimilate knowledge or technology from outside the firm boundary. Cohen and Levinthal's (1989) empirical analysis confirms that R&D has a dual role: in addition to the generation of information and innovations, its function is to enable organisations to understand external developments and to learn from their environment.

This process is not only dependent on the ability of the organisation to access, assimilate and learn, but is also conditional on the types of knowledge being transferred. Much of the knowledge generated by R&D is tacit knowledge, which is difficult to transfer between organisations, as is aptly illustrated by a study of collaboration between Western and Japanese firms. Hamel *et al.* (1989) found that Western companies tended to bring easily imitated technology to a collaboration, whereas Japanese firms' strengths were often 'difficult to unravel' competences which were less transferable. As the example of the alliance between the Rover and Honda car companies has shown, it *is* possible to transfer such knowledge, but this requires very close partnerships over an extended time period.

Collaborations and alliances with other organisations in R&D consortia or joint R&D projects offer opportunities to pursue a wider spread of technologies and access a broader range of expertise than would otherwise be possible, but require experienced and cautious management.

3.6 CAPABILITIES AND CHANGE

Throughout Section 3, first in the discussion sections and then in the Novotel mini-case, we have been exploring what is meant by resources and capabilities and what organisations do with them in practice to implement their strategies and improve their performance.

In the Novotel case you saw an example of how a company had to adjust itself not once, but over and over again, to changes in its business context. Each time it had to review what it was doing, why it was doing it that way and how effective it was relative to what its customers wanted. Novotel's top management had to continually review and monitor its positioning, its hotels, its internal procedures and processes. What at one point in the development of the business had been considered excellent, gradually became average or even substandard as the market developed and customer expectations continued to rise. Costs were rising too; competition was becoming more effective. It was not that the company was doing anything particularly bad, just that capabilities which had been developed under one set of conditions became inappropriate when those conditions changed. This illustrates the 'dynamics' of strategy.

A sense of dynamics is critical in strategy because strategies are always being developed and refined, reviewed and implemented against a set of moving targets which combine every aspect of industry conditions. Industries change, markets change, competitors change or may become partners in certain activities. How these changed industry dynamics and competitive dynamics affect current and future resources and capabilities has already been illustrated in Book 3.

Reflection: the sustainability of resources

In Book 3, you were asked to consider what the 'dynamics' of your own industry had been over the last decade. Had things stayed the same? How had any changes affected the sustainability of your organisation's market position and market share? At this point in our discussion of capabilities and change, think back to your answers to those earlier questions. Now consider the following additional questions:

- Which, if any, of your organisation's resources and capabilities have enabled you to retain or improve your position?
- Which, if any, of your resources or capabilities have been eroded or by-passed?
- Try to explain clearly why and how this has occurred.
- Also try to specify clearly what your organisation has done, or is doing, to refocus or rebuild its resource base.

We are surrounded by examples of this relationship between industry dynamics and competitive dynamics. Charities in the UK have had to rethink their fund-raising procedures, objectives and strategies in the light of competition for the public's charitable purse since the National Lottery was launched by the government. It has been some time since the charities could be adequately managed by inexperienced managers without proper financial or human resource skills and training, or since they could be effectively staffed by altruistic voluntary staff alone. Despite being not-for-profit organisations, they operate in a resource context which is highly competitive (especially for funds) and in which demand often outstrips supply. Similarly, the expectations held by the public of a police service frequently contain political, religious and social subtexts which have affected their relationship with racial or religious minority groups. The recruitment, selection and training of police officers has had to undergo fundamental redesign as a result of changes in the mix of the population, changes in government policy and priorities, and the emergence of entirely new categories of crime (such as computer hacking and sophisticated types of financial fraud) which have necessitated a rebalancing of resources and capabilities fit for such purposes.

Within both local government and national government, changes have been widespread, affecting the fit between changed environment and existing resources and capabilities. For example, within Europe, local government officers have had to develop capabilities which include understanding how the EU functions, in order to respond to the movement of many sources of funding from national government to European Commission departments.

Utilising resources to build capabilities is not a 'once-for-all' exercise. It is a continuous process. What gives this process a sense of direction are the dynamics of the context in which the organisation is trying to survive and succeed. In the next section we will look at some of the ways that organisations try to manage these continuous challenges to success and survival.

4 THE BOUNDARIES OF THE ORGANISATION

Again and again in earlier sections of this book, issues have arisen concerning the ownership of resources. By this we do not just mean who owns particular resources, such as technical knowledge or a patent. More important, in strategic terms, is the question of whether an organisation needs to *own* the resource at all.

The point to emphasise is that organisations do not need to own all the resources they use – they simply need to ensure that they have access to them, together with the *internal* capability to manage them effectively. Therefore, whereas resources may be internal or external to an organisation, *capabilities are always internal.*

Think back once again to the airline take-off and landing slots, or the 'influence' network of the Lebanese chief executive. The organisation needs to ensure merely that the resources it needs are available and secure to be used when it needs them. It is therefore more a matter of 'control' than of ownership. Ownership may be necessary in order to ensure adequacy and frequency of access to a critical resource. Or it may be possible to pay another organisation which owns the resource to rent it to you for a fee instead.

In this section we will discuss the implications of the resource-based view of strategy for the size and scope of organisations. What should they do for themselves and what should they resource from outside? Where should the boundaries be drawn? Does it matter? You may recognise that we are returning to the 'make or buy' (in-source or out-source) issues that we first discussed in Section 3.1. There are also links to the discussion of 'classical', 'sport' and 'relational' contracts in Book 2.

It is useful to indicate the strategy concepts which are relevant here. They include: all corporate-level strategy, transaction cost analysis, time-path dependency and the value chain. These will be discussed in turn.

This section will also look at the consequences of the boundaries of the organisation for managing critical resources effectively, over the long term. That means a consideration of capability-building and the management of learning (i.e. to manage the capability to keep building capabilities).

4.1 CORPORATE STRATEGY ISSUES: ORGANISATIONS OR 'VIRTUAL' ORGANISATIONS?

In Book 1 you were introduced to the three levels of strategy in an organisation. Strategy at the level of the corporation was discussed as the management of the organisation's activities as a corporation, to gain maximum benefit from the organisation as a collection of related or unrelated businesses. At the corporate level lie the strategic decisions affecting the total portfolio of businesses which make up the organisation. It is primarily about the scope of the corporation, its geographic market spread and its product market spread and degree of vertical integration. It therefore defines the industries and markets in which the corporation competes, and the shape of the organisation which will enable it to do so most effectively, by means of the following:

- the overall scope of the organisation
- how it is to be run (its financial and organisational structure)
- how to allocate resources across and between business units
- merger, acquisition, diversification, demerger, divestment decisions affecting the business mix.

This has been a very lively strategy arena for most public-sector and not-for-profit organisations in recent years. Redesign of local authority governing structures has led to some organisations expanding in scope, while others shrink, both in resources and in business mix. Departments and whole authorities have been merged or divested, sometimes as agencies and sometimes as management buy-outs. Similarly, some charities, schools or hospitals are engaged in merger activity to reallocate resources across a wider geographic or market segment. For example, some private schools have merged their boys' and girls' schools to benefit from scale and scope economies – to use their resources more fully and intensively.

4.1.1   Vertical integration or 'quasi-integration'?

These changes have often affected the set of vertical relationships in which the organisation is involved. Many of the set of vertically linked activities in which local government, schools, hospitals or military establishments are involved, are now managed by 'quasi-integration'. Quasi-integration means a long-term relationship that may take the form of a written contract. Alternatively it may take the form of an understanding between the parties as to their mutual expectations. The idea of 'quasi' as opposed to full integration is that you can achieve the same amount of influence or control and the same objectives from organisations without the legal ownership usually implied by vertical integration.

A well-known example of such quasi-integration is that between the UK retailer Marks and Spencer and its suppliers. These are particularly long-standing relationships, many lasting for decades. Although acknowledged as a very demanding customer by its suppliers, these long-term relationships are widely regarded as contributing greatly to the reputation of that company for high-quality products and service. Such a relationship as that between Marks and Spencer and its supplier network is an example of what we defined earlier as a 'virtual' organisation – separate organisations which are dependent upon each other for performing important parts of their activities, and so have many shared interests and resources. Benetton has a similar network of relationships.

The idea contained in the concept of a 'virtual' organisation is that firms are as frequently involved in *collaborative* networking behaviour as in *confrontational* competitive behaviour. Collaboration amongst organisations appears to be increasing rather than diminishing. That is in response to a range of external environmental and internal resource pressures, which are making it difficult for one organisation to contain within its own organisational boundaries all the resources necessary to meet its customers' needs in the long term. For example, there is no car company in the world today which is not involved with one or more of its direct competitors at some point in its value chain. It may be for research into fuel economy, or the design of a new gearbox. These joint ventures and other types of collaborative alliances are partly driven by cost and partly by scarcity of specialist resources. The factors causing such collaboration will be discussed more fully later in the course.

4.1.2   Transaction costs and the scope of the firm

 You should now read pages 374–378 in the Set Book, the sections entitled, 'Economies of scope', 'Economies from internalizing transactions', and 'Information advantages of the diversified corporation'.

Vertical integration forces us to think about some of the most critical strategic issues facing any organisation. We have already discussed them at some length in Section 3.1 in our review of transaction costs. The concept of transaction costs helps us to decide where to draw the boundaries of the organisation and why. For example, Microsoft may be totally reliant on IBM's PC architecture and Intel's chips, but it certainly does not need to own them. By contrast, American Express may wish to keep its IT function in-house rather than to out-source, because it regards its database management capability as a strategic asset and wishes to retain internal control over it. In this case the IT function and systems are regarded not as routine, but as strategic and therefore important not just for current business needs but also for the future development of the business. Table 3.2 summarised the conditions under which either (external) markets or (internal) hierarchies are likely to be preferable in any organisation.

Reflection

In order to be clear about some of the consequences of factors affecting the scope of the firm, compare Novotel's ownership and strategic use of its worldwide reservation systems with SAS's lack of control over its system.

4.2   DYNAMIC CAPABILITIES ISSUES: BUILDING ORGANISATIONAL CAPABILITY

Book 3 discussed the sustainability of resources and capabilities over the longer term, against industry dynamics which affect their long-term viability.

You were asked about the 'dynamics' of your own industry over the last decade and to consider which, if any, of your organisational resources or capabilities had been eroded, and what your organisation is doing to rebuild its resource base. In this section we will look further at such issues as:

- the role of organisational learning and organisational routines in building and sustaining distinctive capabilities
- organisational knowledge flows for sharing knowledge within and between firms.

Miyazaki (1995, pp. 16–17) provides a delightful and simple illustration of the process of building capabilities which will be reproduced here almost in full. She describes the owner of a small café in England who specialises in cooking fried breakfasts including sausage and chips, fried egg and chips, omelette and chips and other similar menu items. His customers are requesting new dishes such as moussaka. The café owner cannot decide which new dish to offer and eventually decides he has no skill in any of them. A friend suggests that he makes a list of what he is good at, that is his capabilities. The list includes:

- purchasing good quality materials such as potatoes, eggs, bread and raw sausages
- producing good quality products at speed, specifically fried eggs, fried chips, grilled sausages and toast
- listening to customers' preferences.

On consideration of this list, he finally has an idea of what to do that will build on his existing capabilities and also develop additional capabilities over time. He will add hamburger with chips and cheese omelette with chips to his menu within two weeks. He has decided that grilling hamburgers is similar to grilling sausages. Also, selecting raw sausages is likely to help him in selecting good raw minced meat. He will have to learn how to season and cook the hamburger, but feels confident that his existing skills in cooking omelettes will enable him to cope with cheese omelettes easily. He also decides that in three months' time he will add moussaka to the menu as a totally new dish which he can practise in his spare time. Some of the skills required to make moussaka, such as frying aubergines, are completely new to him. However, some draw on existing skills, such as chopping onions.

This simple example of capability-building for an individual illustrates the point that capability-building is 'time-path-dependent' and also cumulative – it takes time and effort and needs to build on what has gone before.

Another way of understanding this, for an organisation rather than an individual, is to think of the organisation as a tree. The roots of the tree represent basic resources; the trunk of the tree represents time-path-dependent learning; and the branches represent various capabilities. New branches are always growing and sprouting new leaves, just as organisations should always be able to evolve new capabilities from new combinations of resources and trajectories of learning pathways.

4.2.1 Organisational learning and organisational routines

Learning and innovation is often dependent on what Kay (1993) calls the 'internal architecture' of an organisation, rather than being solely technology- or R&D-dependent. Kay uses the term 'architecture' to describe relationships, both formal and informal, amongst staff (internal networks), with customers and suppliers and inter-firm collaborative arrangements (external networks). Architecture is the conduit for organisational knowledge and routines. The existence of these relationships is not a revelation; in fact they are often taken for granted. This architecture should benefit organizations seeking to obtain economics of scope through the transfer of capabilities across and between different businesses. Indeed, the point is that their importance can easily be overlooked.

Some well-known examples of this type of capability transfer come from the US multinational Procter and Gamble (P&G). The first example is one of transferring a technical capability. As a result of research carried out in Europe in the 1980s for the European market, the formula for a new liquid detergent was so much improved that the technical know-how was transferred to their research centre in the USA and used to improve a similar product already launched in the American market, but not particularly successfully. As a result of the improved research from Europe, P&G's American technical research scientists were able to incorporate improved performance features into the product designed for the US market. The product was subsequently re-launched and became a category leader in its segment. It was the intra-organisational transfer of learning which made this possible.

A second example from P&G concerns its human resource management. As the European market for consumer goods began to change and converge throughout the 1970s and 1980s P&G began to feel it necessary to respond by developing and marketing more Europe-wide products. However, its organisational structure was set up to be autonomous in each European country and the different management teams would not co-operate or share any information. So P&G began to experiment with Europe-wide teams to manage individual products on a Europe-wide basis. To begin with this was a disaster. The 'Euro-teams' were completely ineffectual and were largely ignored in the company. Adjustments were made to the Euro-teams which clarified their remit, enhanced the seniority level and the continuity of membership, and balanced the geographic representativeness of the leaders of each team. It took more than 15 years to make these teams work effectively. However, the company felt that this was an experience curve that it was obliged to travel. It is a learning trajectory that is now being followed and emulated by many rivals.

Some general points on the relationship between organisational learning, organisational routines and capabilities may be noted as follows:

- Capability transfer depends upon organisational learning and organisational routines.
- Knowledge represented by organisational learning will live in the organisation as organisational routines.
- Organisational routines contain both formal and informal, codified and tacit knowledge.

Miyazaki (1995) defines routines as 'patterns of interactions which represent successful solutions to particular problems'.

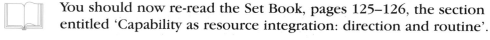 **You should now re-read the Set Book, pages 125–126, the section entitled 'Capability as resource integration: direction and routine'.**

This section in the Set Book discusses mechanisms for integrating and co-ordinating teams of resources, particularly human resource skills and knowledge. Two integrating mechanisms are discussed: rules and directives, and organisational routines. The first type is based on codified knowledge. The second type is based on 'regular and predictable patterns of activity made up of a sequence of co-ordinated actions by individuals' (Grant, p. 125). This implies that organisational routines involve a high degree of tacit knowledge. The role of management is to enable the development of routines to achieve integration and co-ordination of capabilities, just as in the P&G examples.

Organisational learning, and knowledge flows within firms, together with other process issues in strategy will be discussed further in Book 6.

Activity 4.1 _____

Describe any 'organisational routines' (explicit or implicit) within your organisation for:

- building
- exploiting
- transferring or sharing
- sustaining
- blocking organisational capabilities.

4.3   OWNERSHIP, CONTROL OR JUST LINKS IN A CHAIN?

This discussion of the boundaries of the firm ends by revisiting the value chain. It is one of the simplest ways to understand the issue of where to draw organisational boundaries. The boundaries of the firm are synonymous with the decisions it has taken in constructing its value chain. One of the ways of understanding the range of strategic options available to an organisation is to see where it has chosen to cut its activities along the value chain. How vertically integrated has it chosen to be and why? This is the balance it has chosen between internal capabilities and external complementary assets.

Hall (1994) defines a functional capability as resulting from 'the knowledge, skill and experience of employees and others in the value chain'. Each value chain configuration embodies a different set of such knowledge and experience.

Go back once more to Figure 3.2, the Novotel business chain. Ask yourself whether it is necessary for Novotel to own its own worldwide central reservation system, situated outside Paris. It could access another reservation system, possibly the Sabre system belonging to American Airlines. Perhaps, in the view of Novotel's management, ownership of their own system (in fact it is owned by the parent company Accor) confers upon them the ability to construct other linkages within the firm or across the other chains in the Accor group of businesses. It makes it possible to transfer learning or enhance customer service or develop more targeted marketing initiatives. For Novotel this may be a resource on which they have built distinctive capabilities. They have chosen to construct their value chain in this way rather than another way. Their specific value chain configuration forms the basis of their competitive strategy. It is likely to be different from the configuration of other international hotel chains.

Similarly, if we return now to Benetton and consider once more the manufacturing and retail value chains in Figures 1.2 and 1.3, Benetton's sources of distinctiveness are clear. The boundaries of the two organisations, Novotel and Benetton, represent particular management decisions about how to design their value chains to maximise their respective potential sources of advantage and appropriate the best returns from that particular pattern of activities.

5 SUMMARY AND CONCLUSION

In this book we have emphasised a number of things about the resource-based approach to strategy:

- that resources form the basis of capabilities
- that strategy analysis must include the identification of the cluster of resources of each organisation
- the notion of 'ownership' by organisations of distinctive capabilities, i.e. those which are unique to that organisation
- capabilities (to meet your organisation's objectives) are likely to be internal and owned, whereas resources may be either internal or external (not owned)
- that distinctive capabilities generate potential returns for the firm if they are sustainable and the returns are appropriable
- that it is from these distinctive capabilities that the variance of performance between firms in the same industry sector arises
- that the depreciation of resources (and the returns earned from them) necessitates the replenishment and upgrading of resources
- that organisational routines provide the basis for the exchange of skills, expertise and learning
- the role of innovation in enabling capabilities
- that human resources are critical in the resource-based approach to strategy
- that it is managers and managerial action which hold the key to creating organisational distinctiveness through building, developing and renewing capabilities.

This book has emphasised the following:

- the ability to exploit clusters of resources to create and accumulate new strategic assets more quickly and cheaply than competitors
- the organisational dynamics of identifying, building and sustaining non-tradable, non-imitable capabilities
- the organisational dynamics and routines to enable the application of capabilities, e.g. to innovation or to learning.

5.1 OBJECTIVES REVISITED

The purpose of this book has been to explore with you the resource-based approach to strategic thinking and strategic decision-making. Having completed your work on this book, you should be able to state the difference between a resource and a capability. More important, however, is that you have also learned from this book the difference between the two matters, and why, therefore, they are such powerful concepts in strategic thinking. It is your task as managers to transform your organisation's resources into the capabilities that will be the source of its future strengths.

REFERENCES

Amit, R. and Schoemaker, P. (1993) 'Strategic assets and organisational rents', *Strategic Management Journal*, Vol. 14, pp. 33–46.

Baden-Fuller, C., Calori, R. and Hunt, B. (1995) 'Novotel Case Study'.

Barney, J.B. (1991) 'Firm resources and sustained competitive advantage', *Journal of Management*, Vol. 17, No. 1, pp. 99–120.

Bartlett, C.A. and Ghoshal, S. (1993) 'Beyond the M-form: toward a managerial theory of the firm', *Strategic Management Journal*, Vol. 14, Special Issue, Winter, pp. 23–46.

Chandler, A.D. (1962) *Strategy and Structure*, MIT Press, Cambridge, MA.

Cohen, W.M. and Levinthal, D.A. (1989) 'Innovation and learning: the two faces of R&D – implications for the analysis of R&D investment', *The Economic Journal*, Vol. 99 pp. 569–596.

Daft, R. (1983) *Organisation Theory and Design*, West, New York.

Grant, R.M. (1991) 'The resource-based theory of competitive advantage: implications for strategy formulation', *California Management Review*, Spring, pp. 114–135.

Grant, R.M. (1995) *Contemporary Strategy Analysis: concepts, techniques, applications*, 3rd edn, Blackwell, Oxford (the Set Book).

Hall, R. (1994) 'A framework for identifying the intangible sources of sustainable competitive advantage' in Hamel, G. and Heene, A. (eds) *Competence-Based Competition*, J. Wiley & Sons, Chichester.

Hamel, G., Doz, Y.L. and Prahalad, C.K. (1989) 'Collaborate with your competitors – and win', *Harvard Business Review,* January–February pp. 133–139.

Hofer, C.W. and Schendel, D. (1978) *Strategy Formulation: analytical concepts*, West Publishing Co., St. Paul, MN.

Kay, J. (1993) *Foundations of Corporate Success*, Oxford University Press, Oxford.

Lippman, S.A. and Rumelt, R.P. (1982) 'Uncertain imitability: an analysis of inter-firm differences in efficiency under competition', *The Bell Journal of Economics*, Vol. 13, No. 2, pp. 418–438.

Miyazaki, K. (1995) *Building Competences in the Firm: lessons from Japanese and European optoelectronics*, St Martin's Press, New York.

Nelson, R. and Winter, S.G. (1982) *An Evolutionary Theory of Economic Change,* The Belknap Press, Cambridge, MA.

Nonaka, I. (1991) 'The knowledge-creating company', *Harvard Business Review*, November–December, pp. 96–104.

Pavitt, K. (1989) *What do we Know about the Usefulness of Science: the case for diversity*, DRC Discussion paper No. 65, Science Policy Research Unit, University of Sussex.

Peteraf, M. (1993) 'The cornerstones of competitive advantage: a resource-based view', *Strategic Management Journal*, Vol. 14, pp. 179–191.

Polyani, M. (1966) *The Tacit Dimension*, Doubleday, New York.

Porter, M.E. (1985) *Competitive Advantage*, The Free Press, New York.

Prahalad, C.K. and Hamel, G. (1990) 'The core competence of the corporation', *Harvard Business Review*, May–June, pp. 71–91.

Quinn, J.B. (1992) *Intelligent Enterprise*, The Free Press, New York.

Rumelt, R. (1984) 'Toward a strategic theory of the firm' in Lamb, R. (ed.) *Competitive Strategic Management*, Prentice-Hall, Englewood Cliffs, NJ.

Rumelt, R. (1991) 'How Much Does Industry Matter?' *Strategic Management Journal*, Vol. 12, No. 3, pp. 167–185.

Schumpeter, J.A. (1934) *The Theory of Economic Development*, Harvard University Press, Cambridge, MA.

Segal-Horn, S. (1995) 'Core competence and international strategy in service multinationals' in Armistead, C. and Teare, R. (eds) *Services Management: new directions and perspectives*, Cassell, London.

Stopford, J. and Baden-Fuller, C. (1990) 'Corporate rejuvenation', *Journal of Management Studies*, Vol. 27, No. 4, pp. 399–415.

Teare, R. and Armistead, C. (1995) *Services Management: New directions, new perspectives*, Cassell, London.

Teece, D. (1980) 'Economies of scope and the scope of the enterprise', *Journal of Economic Behaviour and Organisation*, Vol. 1, No. 3, pp. 223–247.

Teece, D. (1982) 'Towards an economic theory of the multiproduct firm', *Journal of Economic Behaviour and Organisation*, Vol. 3, pp. 39–63.

Teece, D., Pisano, G. and Shuen, A. (1990) 'Firm capabilities, resources and the concept of strategy', University of California Working Paper EAP-38.

Williamson, O.E. (1975) *Markets and Hierarchies*, The Free Press, New York.

ACKNOWLEDGEMENTS

Grateful acknowledgement is made to the following sources for permission to reproduce material in this book:

Figures

Figure 2.1: Peteraf, M. A. and Kellogg, J. L. (1993) 'The cornerstones of competitive advantage: A resource-based view', Figure 3, in Schendel, D. (1993), *Strategic Management*, **14**(3), March 1993, Copyright 1993 by John Wiley & Sons, Ltd. Reprinted by permission of John Wiley & Sons Ltd; *Figure 3.1:* Grant, R. M. (1995) *Contemporary Strategy Analysis*, 2nd edition, Figure 5.10, Basil Blackwell Ltd; *Figure 3.2:* Teare, R. and Armistead, C. (1995) *Services Management: new directions, new perspectives*, Figure 1, Cassell PLC; *Figure 3.3:* Baden-Fuller, C. 1995, 'Strategic innovations, corporate entrepreneurship and matching outside-in to inside-out approaches to strategy research', *British Journal of Management*, **6**, December 1995, © 1995 by John Wiley & Sons Ltd. Reproduced by permission of John Wiley & Sons Ltd.

Table

Table 3.3: Bartlett, C. A. and Ghoshal, S. (1993) 'Beyond the M-Form: toward a managerial theory of the firm', Figure 2, in Schendel, D., Cyert, R. M. and Williams, J. R. (1993) *Strategic Management*, **14**, Winter 1993, Copyright 1993 by John Wiley & Sons, Ltd. Reprinted by permission of John Wiley & Sons Ltd.

Photographs

Page 17: The Guide Dogs for the Blind Association; *Page 20:* M. and C. Saatchi; *Page 36:* Buckfast Abbey, Buckfastleigh.